DEVELOPING THE
LEADER'S
HEART

How Jesus Shaped **12 Men** in **3 Years** to **Change the World**

DR. BILL LAWRENCE

TABLE OF CONTENTS

INTRODUCTION

More than 2,000 years ago, twelve unlikely men laid the foundation for a movement that has transformed cultures, impacted generations, brought down governments, overcome all efforts to destroy it and endures to this day.

No other men in history have changed the world as these twelve did. Because of their commitment, billions of people have entrusted their lives to their message, walked away from fame and fortune for their cause and died for their truth. They had neither power, position, nor pedigree, yet their movement has flourished through the ages.

How did these powerless men wield such power?

They followed Jesus, who called the future leaders of His mission to follow in even the most challenging of His footsteps. This required a new focus—the process of leader formation.

In the Gospels, we see that Jesus never taught His men leadership skills, such as how to develop a vision statement or build an organizational chart. Instead, He spent months with them, calling them to a new and better way that could only be learned by following Him.

Jesus transformed His leaders by loving them, modeling for them and teaching them a ***series of realities*** so they could respond to His call to take up the cross—not once, but continually.

This is not a book about steps, lists, switches or how I did it. It is not a self-help manual. Rather, this is a book about how Jesus formed leaders, a process that is untried and untested by many. Not surprisingly, Jesus produced extraordinary and lasting results. *Leader Formation* echoes Christ's ancient call for leaders to be shaped through the power of the cross.

Jesus established a movement that has endured across cultures and generations. His methods take us into new depths of our own hearts as we advance His movement into the 21st century and beyond. In the pages ahead, we will see how Jesus worked in the hearts and lives of His first followers as He formed them into the founders of His movement—a movement that has moved from its primary base to blanket the globe.

CHAPTER 1

THE HEART OF LEADERSHIP

"For man looks at the outward appearance, but the Lord looks at the heart." (1 Samuel 16:7)

Have you ever wondered why you are a leader?

Most people would assume they are in a leadership role because of their gifting, skills and abilities. The fact is, you are a leader because God called you to be a leader. In other words, you play a vital part in God's plan for those whom you influence because throughout all of history, God has accomplished His purposes through the leaders He has raised up.

Do you realize that God's call to leadership is a holy call? It is a special call from God to you, and He wants to use you to make a difference in the hearts of those you influence. Without your influence, they will not become the men and women He wants them to be.

What greater privilege could you have? It doesn't matter whether you have limited or major leadership responsibility. What matters is that you fulfill it according to the way God is forming you. The end result is that you make a difference in others whom He is calling you to influence.

The High Calling of a Leader

As we prepare to take a look at how Jesus formed monumental leaders out of a ragtag bunch in just three short years, we begin to see that leadership is much less important to God and His kingdom than the actual person to whom God has given the responsibility to be His kind of leader.

The truth is, leadership has never been easy—and "more training" isn't the magic bullet.

When we think everything that could be written on leadership has been penned, works still keep coming. Yet decade after decade, leadership surprisingly has not changed. And why? Largely because there is a massive gap between the aspirations and expectations of leadership and the reality which we see. We presume the issue behind our unmet resolve is a matter of training and experience while the heart of the leader is often overlooked.

In the U.S. alone, companies spend an estimated $31 billion annually on leadership development.[1] Executive leadership programs at top universities help prepare future leaders with the latest strategies. Yet,

---

1. "Leadership Awakened," Deloitte University Press, https://dupress.deloitte.com/dup-us-en/focus/human-capital-trends/2016/identifying-future-business-leaders-leadership.html, Feb. 29, 2016.

with all of our learning, leadership failure is much more prevalent than success.

The truth is, leadership has never been easy—and "more training" isn't the magic bullet. In fact, it can get in the way of God's intended purposes.

Throughout this book, we'll discuss topics you'll never read in a typical leadership book—but I promise you, the concepts we will consider will renew your passion for leading Jesus' way and help you realize that leadership skills alone are not sufficient to fulfill your calling.

If you want to impact lives around you, the initial change must begin in you.

Leadership is failing today just like it has for thousands of years because it still overlooks the heart. Even when we have accomplished everything we can to pursue leadership, we still have few real leaders and often poor ones at that.

Why is it that talent, experience and success cannot produce effective leaders? Consider this from Barbara Kellerman, who became the founding executive director of the Harvard Kennedy School's Center for Public Leadership. In *The End of Leadership*,

Kellerman draws some insightful conclusions when she states that leaders are "in disrepute":

> "...The tireless teaching of leadership has brought us no closer to leadership nirvana than we were previously...we don't have much better an idea of how to grow good leaders, or how to stop or slow bad leaders, than we did a hundred or even a thousand years ago. Not withstanding the enormous sums of money and time that have been poured into trying to teach people how to lead, over its roughly forty-year history, the leadership industry has not in any major, meaningful, measurable way improved the human condition." [2]

Dr. Kellerman summarizes these thoughts with this statement:

> "While the leadership industry has been thriving—growing and prospering beyond anyone's early imaginings—leaders by and large are performing poorly, worse in many ways than before, miserably disappointing in any case to those among us who once believed the experts held the keys to the kingdom." [3]

Everywhere we look we see talented men and women who occupy positions of influence but cannot unite their followers or move them forward. Some of them know the mechanics of leadership and do

2. Kellerman, Barbara. *The End of Leadership*, p. 7, e-edition, iBook, HarperCollins, n.d.
3. Ibid., pp. 7-8.

all the right things, yet it often turns out the wrong way. They make promises they cannot keep and refuse to face their own failures or open the way for better leaders. They may be full of great ideas, wonderful words and the right steps, but they are not successful leaders. There's a missing dimension in their lives, something far more foundational than the ability to lead.

It's All About to Change

Throughout the Old Testament, we see a series of leader failures and very few successful leaders. How was God going to address this issue in the New Testament when the only way He could start and sustain His church was through the leaders He called? Leadership as we know it was about to fundamentally change. God would have to form His leaders in a whole new way.

As a matter of fact, if you allow it, it is about to change you. As you read on, I hope you will not see leadership in the way you once did. With God's help, you will step into a process of leader formation that will change you and the people around you in an unprecedented way. You are about to discover that:

The Heart of the Leader is the Heart of Leadership

Open your heart to Him now. Allow His grace to begin a fresh work in you. May God prepare you and shape you into a transformative leader—for the sake of those you lead—to multiple generations.

CHAPTER 2

THREE YEARS TO CHANGE THE WORLD

"…Christ in us, the hope of glory." (Colossians 1:17)

Three Years to Change the World

Let's suppose that in the next three years you must lead the way into a magnetic, self-sustaining, energizing and engaging movement demanding total dedication. You must choose a handful of people, all of whom you currently do not know. This movement must reach every corner of the globe in local languages and cultures, and bring about radical changes in relationships, commitments and values. This thrust must continue increasingly and indefinitely across social and generational lines for as long as the world exists.

What would be the most effective way to create such a movement in three short years that would literally change the world?

One idea would be to scour the earth for the best world-class leaders you can attract by challenging them with your vision and organizing them to be completely focused on your aim.

You would raise the resources you need, create a quality control structure, meet to keep them accountable, evaluate the process, make changes and press ahead. You would develop a great vision statement, define values, generate a catchy tagline, build an attention-getting digital strategy and create extensive detailed plans so everyone knows exactly what to do.

These plans would enable you to make certain that everything is being accomplished while enabling you to stay in control. Then you could teach as many people as possible the skills of leadership that are vital for the effectiveness of the movement. You would hold conferences, conduct seminars and workshops, start leadership schools and make certain everyone has the skills necessary to lead. How could you lose with this kind of strategy, right?

The reality is, you *could* do all of this, but you *would* fail because you cannot create a movement through these means that will reach the world or last for millennia.

How Jesus Formed Leaders

More than 1000 years after Israel was granted their wish for a king—Jesus, the King of Kings—turned the world upside down with a new kind of leadership. When Jesus came on the scene He revealed the importance of the heart. He began focusing on the heart disease of these unlikely leaders and created a movement that would change the world—not by enrolling them in a leadership development program, but by performing open heart surgery.

It was a radically different leadership style. Contrary to what we might expect, it wasn't about leadership development; it was about leader formation. The very good news is that He invites us to be part of this movement today and He moves in us and through us to form us into the kind of leader who can accomplish His purposes in our day.

Jesus called unqualified followers.

Jesus called unqualified followers. Think about it: Peter, Andrew, James, John, Matthew... and *Judas*. Really? How could anyone possibly start an eternal movement with men like these? Why didn't He at least try to get men who were qualified to lead? They were un-teachable, competitive, driven and power-seeking. They had hardened hearts and thick heads.

Why did Jesus think these men could lead a movement around the corner, let alone around the world? He knew they were not up to the task and said as much on the night of His arrest when He told them they would all fall away when the Roman soldiers came for Him. He knew they didn't have the strength to stand against Rome and risk their lives, yet He called and formed them anyway.

He made His whole movement dependent on them. If they failed, His movement would have failed. The fact that He called these men makes no sense—it is upside-down thinking. None of us would consider such men for our cause, right?

Why did He call these utterly *unqualified* followers? Because they were the only kind He had to call.

No one is qualified to lead the Jesus movement—and that is just as true today as it was then. Throughout history no one has started out as a qualified leader for Jesus because we all are unworthy servants at best (see Luke 17:10). Yet Jesus continues to call the unqualified and the unworthy to do the supernatural. Amazing!

Does this mean that because Jesus didn't focus on leadership practices we shouldn't either?

No. I am not saying we should disregard competence in forming leaders, but I am saying we should stop ignoring character and the heart as much as we do.

Remember, the disciples were experienced businessmen who already had the skills they needed to run a successful fishing enterprise on the shores of Galilee when Jesus called them. More significantly, they had a much deeper need, and that is where Jesus concentrated His energy.

The Missing Heart

If we want to produce truly lasting results, we must take an entirely different approach. Even though it makes no sense, we must do what Jesus did. What He did is innately contrary to all our instincts, countercultural in every respect, seemingly certain to fail—yet it succeeds whenever and wherever it is done.

Jesus' greatest concern for His disciples, the one thing He knew could cause them to fail was *His leaders' hearts*. Their hearts were hardened, and He had to often confront them with that fact. They had hearts filled with a passion for power, success and control, hearts that needed to be transformed by Christ's power from hardness to brokenness. Tasked with developing the team that would change the world, Jesus focused His attention primarily on the hearts of His men. What is the missing dimension in leadership today, the one element that will prevent leaders from accomplishing all God has for them?

It is an *altared heart*, a heart fully committed to God and placed on His altar as a living sacrifice. The greatest challenge about being a living sacrifice is how easy it is to get up off the altar. Putting our hearts on God's altar is not something we do from time to time—but continually, as we daily take up the cross and grow more and more into the likeness of Christ.

When it comes to Christian leadership:

The heart of the leader is the heart of leadership.

The idea of "heart" in the Bible is rooted deeply in the Old Testament. It is a Hebrew concept, and to the Hebrews the heart was far more than the place and source of the emotions. To the ancient chroniclers, poets and prophets of the Old Testament, the heart was everything we are apart from our bodies, the deepest core of our being, everything that makes us who we are. In other words, our total identity. The heart is not just our emotional center but our personal center, the very essence of who we are.

We have leaders with talent, experience and success, leaders trained to think and do leadership— but unless their hearts are transformed, they will take a great fall and perhaps never recover. As Christians, the most common factor that keeps us from fulfilling God's call in our lives is the decision to depend on our skills for leadership. Only desperate dependence on Jesus enables leaders to accomplish their true role in leadership as He uses their gifts and experience to accomplish His purposes.

Christ's kind of leaders recognize that their success is not the issue. What matters is the glory of God and the good of Christ's kingdom. Christlikeness, not self, becomes the driving force of leadership.

The heart is not just our emotional center but our personal center, the very essence of who we are.

Such leaders will be able to exercise Christlike leadership because of what Christ has done within their heart. Only a transformed leader can accomplish leadership that produces eternal impact.

From the Functional to the Foundational

There are two levels of leadership: the functional and the foundational. Talent, experience, success and the skills needed to accomplish them form the functional level of leadership, the make-it-happen, get-it-done level. We are right to depend on these elements to pursue the functional, but we cannot depend on them for the totality of our leadership.

> **Only a transformed leader can accomplish leadership that produces eternal impact.**

As leaders we are building eternal impact through our service—and that must depend not only on the effective functioning of our head and hands, but also on the foundation of eternal enablement through our hearts.

The heart is the foundational element of leadership within us that the head and hands depend on to make an eternal difference for Christ. The heart is the track that our leadership skills run on. When this foundation is jeopardized, our leadership falls short as we rely increasingly on methods to do what only a transformed heart can accomplish. The functions of leadership carried out through the head and the hands will fail when it lacks the foundation of a transformed heart.

We must focus on the heart of the leader, the heart progressively placed on God's altar in constantly renewed and deeper ways until it is ultimately transformed for God's glory through the cross.

A leader who has a wonderfully loving heart, pursues all the spiritual disciplines, and has great character but lacks competence is ineffective. While skills are essential but not sufficient, so also is the right heart alone insufficient. Leaders need both competence and character, so we must grow and teach others in how to think and communicate (the head), and how to lead (the hands), but at the core we must focus on the heart to form the foundation of a leader.

> **The heart is the track that our leadership skills run on.**

This focus on the heart runs contrary to modern leadership development, which spends most of its time in leadership training on developing skills. The fact that this is man's default both makes sense and falls short for two basic reasons:

1. The pressure to get things done demands skill, so we move to accomplish the task and overlook character and the deeper issues of the human heart.

2. Competence is much easier to form than character, and knowledge is easier to deal with than our identity; therefore, we tend to focus on skills at the cost of our hearts. When we

build on too small a foundation, our leadership totters just one hardship away from eventual collapse.

The Results Gap

As leaders, many times we experience a results gap—the distance between our expectations and accomplishments. While we think of this as failure, God views it as a stop along the way. Often the results gap is self-imposed, a self-determined standard we establish as a way of measuring our success that is not of God.

Such a standard usually involves our superiority—the demonstration that we're really good at what we do, we're number one, the best.

God does not care if we're the best. There's only one King—and He reigns supreme. Such measurements are irrelevant to God. All they do is depress us and make us feel like failures.

However, the results gap is something He needs to take us through, so He lets us fall into a personal sinkhole and allows us to stay there until we are ready to respond to Him and move forward.

Think of when Jesus called Peter "Satan" (see Matthew 16:23) or when Peter denied Christ (see Luke 22:54-62). These were failures in Peter's life, and to us failure is final. Failure to God, however, is an expected and even necessary event in our pilgrimage toward impact and fruitfulness.

Without the failure of thinking like Satan, Peter never would have known the call of the cross. Without the failure of denying Christ, Peter never would have experienced the healing restoration of Christ's commission of him. It was through the results gap that Peter was broken and then made whole.

So it is with us: We must fail in order to become effective. It's all part of learning that head and hands are not sufficient—*only an altared heart can make us adequate for God's call in our lives.*

Sometimes the results gap becomes a black, closed, confusing place... seemingly with no way out. In other words, like death. That's because it *is* death.

There are times when God decides we've pursued our number-one focus long enough, and we need to move to the place where He can use us. We must die to being first and rise to being last, willing to give our lives to serve Him instead of using God's words to mask our drive to serve our interests in Jesus's name. He closes us in until we are ready to cry out to Him the way Jonah did from the belly of the fish (see Jonah 2).

Then He does the same thing with us that He did with Jonah, Peter and countless others: He brings us to the place of the altared heart, the place of maximum power and fruitfulness. And remember from the last chapter, the early exception becomes the lasting rule.

Whenever a person's capabilities become the central focus, you can expect to see failure.

The Altared Heart

Jesus had only three years to turn Galilean fishermen—working-class men with no formal theological education, polish or privilege—into world-class leaders. Yet He focused primarily on one element in their lives: their hearts.

He knew the rest would take care of itself, but not the heart. It has to be cultivated, broken and altared if the head and the hands are to reach their true potential.

Passing through the results gap and emerging with altared hearts is exactly how Peter, James, John and the rest of the disciples became the great leaders Jesus created them to be. He called for them to place their hearts on His altar by taking up the cross and denying self so He could bring them into the greatness of His plan for them. He transformed who they were so they could do what He wanted them to do.

The process they went through is the same process we must go through.

How can you be the very best leader possible?

The only way you and I can reach the heights Jesus has for us is to begin the same process of transformation that Jesus took the disciples through. Not all who start will be willing to finish, but those who do will experience Christ's power to achieve His supernatural purposes "...Christ in us, the hope of glory" (Colossians 1:27).

In the upcoming chapters, we will focus on seven realities that Jesus used to form His disciples. These are the core concepts that form the essence of this book. My prayer for you is that these realities will take hold of your heart and give you a fresh vision for leadership. My hope is that you will allow Christ to form in you the same things He formed in the disciples and prepare you for unparalleled leadership.

May God bless you as you read on and discover the journey of leader formation.

CHAPTER 3

IT'S IMPOSSIBLE

"...without me you can do nothing." (John 15:5)

The stage is set. Jesus has chosen twelve unlikely men to change the world. In three years these "unskilled" followers will change history—and become leaders who, for centuries to come, men and women will want to emulate. Jesus is about to begin Leadership 101 with the most mind-blowing miracle His disciples have witnessed—and He chooses to involve them because He knows it will forever shape them and transform their dependence on Him.

<u>You</u> Give Them Something to Eat

For the disciples it happened on a hillside surrounded by 5,000 men, plus women and children. The twelve were fresh off a ministry assignment in which Jesus had sent them into towns and villages throughout Israel to show them what He could do through them. They returned with stories of great success. Their confidence was high.

At the same time, John the Baptist had just been beheaded. Jesus knew His hour was coming too. It was time for Him to focus on preparing His men for the supernatural tasks that lay ahead. He sought out a solitary place to withdraw with them where He could teach them the things they must learn. But the crowd kept coming. Because of what the disciples had done, more people than ever wanted to see and hear Jesus. They followed them by the thousands to listen to His teaching as He fed them with God's word.

The hour was late, the day was long, and the people were hungry. Dinnertime was fast approaching, and the disciples were becoming restless. Most of the people had a long way to go to get to their homes and food. If they didn't leave now, the old and the young, the weak and the needy, would not make it. They were in a wilderness, and these people needed to be sent on their way for their own good. As much as they could feed their spirits on the Lord's words, His wisdom could never fill their bellies. Only bread could do that.

The disciples must have conferred and decided to interrupt Jesus to point out the problem. It was not like Him to miss seeing the needs of others—no one had more compassion for the crowds than He did (Mark 6:34). So they gave Him a quick reminder that it was time to wrap things up and send the crowd home.

Jesus' reply to their interruption startled and confused them. "They don't need to go away," he told them. "You give them something to eat" (Mark 6:37). Note: Jesus did not say, "We will give them something to eat." He said, "YOU do it." *What?* How could they do that? They didn't even have food for themselves.

The disciples were ready for the church service to be over. They were looking forward to getting away from the crowd and retreating to the green room to relax with Jesus. Jesus' response stunned them. Then He moved from His absurd command and asked what certainly appeared to be a senseless question: "How many loaves do you have?" Without giving them any opportunity to respond, he forcefully directed them to *"Go and see!"*

Why did He send them to discover the obvious impossibility of the situation? Nothing He was doing made sense. They knew they didn't have enough bread to feed these hungry people, probably close to 20,000 in all, and so did He. Did He issue this command to make them feel foolish and futile, calling attention to the problem by sending them through the crowd to ask if they had food?

No. *He wanted His disciples to discover how little they had. He wanted to make their lack of resources utterly undeniable. He wanted them to face their inadequacy square in the face.* He needed them to hit a wall.

Have you ever hit a wall like this—where everything you had to give was nowhere near enough for the challenges you faced?

There was no way to carry out His directive, but the disciples had no other choice but to humbly obey. They returned to Him with five loaves and two fish and challenged Him, "What is that among so many?" Jesus then told them to have the people sit down and prepare to eat (John 6:9-10). Talk about awkward. How much confidence in your leader would you have to have to obey this command?

As the disciples did their work, Jesus openly gave thanks for a pitiful amount of food, and then proceeded, with the disciples' help, to feed all of the people with food to spare. *All of the people.*

The disciples were perplexed by their insufficiency, while Jesus thanked God for it.

The disciples were perplexed by their insufficiency, while Jesus thanked God for it.

You see, Jesus had three years to create a movement to change the world, and He started building His future leaders through an impossible situation. He had to teach them that they were inadequate for what He was calling them to do. This was Jesus' leadership lesson for them that day on that sprawling hillside along the Sea of Galilee.

Without Me You Can Do Nothing

The same is true today. Leadership begins where we least expect it—with our inadequacy. This is exactly what the disciples faced when Jesus made His supernatural demand of them. You see, Jesus was very clear when He said, "...without Me you can do nothing." (John 15:5)

> **Our cry of desperation is exactly what He wants to hear from us.**

But do we take Him seriously? We often struggle to believe it and try everything we can to prove Him wrong. From time to time we are forced to accept this truth and we cry out for His help—and He comes through. Then we return to serving Him in our own strength, and once again we arrive back at a place of utter helplessness.

Have you ever been there—completely overwhelmed by situations where you are coming up short? Maybe you feel like a complete failure. I've been there—and I have good news for you. When we humbly face our inadequacies and acknowledge that without Him "we can do nothing," we are exactly where God wants us to be: facing our inadequacy and completely depending on Him.

No amount of training or education qualifies us to do God's will. Our cry of desperation is exactly what He wants to hear from us. It is the starting point to getting serious about becoming the leader He called us to be.

This leads us to the first reality of altared leadership...

Principle #1:
The Reality of Leader Inadequacy

You must do what you cannot do with what you do not have
for the rest of your lives.

The Wall of Inadequacy

Jesus deliberately leads us into situations we cannot overcome in order to teach us this foundational leadership principle: ***You must do what you cannot do with what you do not have for the rest of your lives.***

Sometimes in our lives we go through seasons like the disciples did when they were first sent out by Jesus—great results and one blessing after another. Our confidence in Him grows, and we realize that we are able to serve the Lord after all, despite our doubts. Then, to our surprise, everything that has been working stops working. We hit an invisible wall, and no matter what we do, it blocks our way.

We ask ourselves, *Where did that wall come from?* Then we try to figure out how to get through it, but there is no doorway. So we attempt to climb over it, but we can't get to the top. The wall is insurmountable. Jesus has brought us to a dead-end.

This is the wall of inadequacy, the barrier we cannot overcome that sets our insufficiency undeniably before us. The Lord lets us strive to overcome this wall. He lets us search for what works, to do everything possible to feed the 5,000. We go in search of any resource we can find but return with short supply. We consult with other leaders, read books and go to conferences looking for solutions, only to fail. With each new idea we end up back at the same old wall. There is no solution. Once we hit the wall of inadequacy, we will never get away from it.

What wall are you facing today?

- A situation that is unfair?
- A circumstance you cannot change?
- A relationship you cannot heal?
- A problem you cannot solve?

Are you condemned to spend your life hunkered down against that wall, trying to make failure look like success, wearing cover-up smiles full of fading glory?

The reality is, we see the limits of what we have, but God sees the opportunity because of what He has. To become His kind of leaders, we must allow Him to shape our hearts. He wants to prepare us to carry on His movement—unqualified, inadequate, stunned by His command, incapable of doing what He wants and unable to deny it.

To lead for Jesus is not only to feel inadequate; it is to *be* inadequate.

Let me drive home this point: *If you are looking for a way to feel adequate in serving or leading for Christ, you have completely missed the point of what leadership for Him means.*

You are not doing what He wants you to do; you are doing what you want to do in His name because you have reduced His demand to the level of your resources. You have done what Jesus would not let His disciples do: You have gotten rid of the crowd. You have reduced the 5,000 to five: a small, intimate handful of snackers who can be satisfied with the few crumbs you can distribute, and you are calling that the Jesus kind of leadership.

To lead for Jesus is not only to feel inadequate; it is to *be* inadequate. It is to be thankful for what we have when it is not enough. Why? Because He will never give us something we can do. Never! Jesus can only give us things to do that He alone can do—and this will never change, no matter how much education, experience or expertise we gain.

This is why we must never forget this core reality of the altared heart: *You must do what you cannot do with what you do not have for the rest of your life.* This is the reality of leader inadequacy.

Coming to the Wall

I remember the first time I hit the wall as a leader. I was a young pastor in San Jose, California, knee deep into a building process for a campus we desperately needed. We had done our due diligence and managed our plans with a fine-toothed comb. We had appealed to the congregation, and they responded. We were within $10,000 of our need, and our confidence was high as we stepped into our elder's retreat to go over some of the details for our building plans.

Our elders were a group of high-caliber leaders—several of whom had helped us plant the church just 9 years prior. We enjoyed a great time of worship and prayer before getting down to business. As the meeting came together, our board chairman, a district manager for a major utility company with over 1,100 people reporting to him, led the meeting. He was a controlled man and one of the most respected leaders in the church. He spoke: "Fellas," he said, and then he started to cry. We knew this wasn't a good sign.

In spite of all that could be done, the building costs had increased by $100,000. Now, this was in 1977. In today's money, that was a million-dollar spike in costs. We simply did not have the funds—and yet we had to begin building as soon as possible because the lease on our meeting facility could not be renewed, and we had nowhere else to meet. We were at an impossible impasse. We had hit a wall.

I remember finding myself in tears on my knees. Not only were we in an impossible place, but I felt responsible for leading us there. In reality, God was doing heart surgery on me. He was forming me as a leader. He knew we would be $100,000 short, yet He led me into it. He was bringing me to the point of utter dependence. There was no way for us to meet this need. We could not go backward, and we could not go forward. I stood, as a leader, at the wall of inadequacy.

Embracing Inadequacy

"*You* give them something to eat!" The command of Jesus comes ringing down from that Galilean hillside to the Santa Clara Valley of California, to you and me today. He has never changed His command, and He never will. "How many loaves do you have? *Go and see!*"

Jesus is as clear to His leaders today as He was on that late afternoon—and His leaders felt just as helpless then as we do now.

What is His reason? For us to see what we do have so we know with assurance what we don't have. We should be grateful for our lack because when we've reached this point of inadequacy, it sends us to our knees. We become aware of our extreme limitations and of God's supernatural ability to meet every need.

Do you have experience? Do you have a network? Do you have opportunity? Do you have education? Do you have money? Maybe not. But now you know what you do have: five loaves and two fish. Now you also know what you don't have: enough to feed 5,000. And most of all, now you know that you cannot do what Jesus commands you to do with what you have. Still, His command stands:

You must do what you cannot do with what you do not have for the rest of your life!

That is where I stood with the elders of our church when we faced an impossible need and had to give up all thought of our adequacy. What were we going to do? Lord, what are You going to do? This is the question we faced in that overwhelming moment.

While I will share more about the outcome in the next chapter, it is critical to understand how, looking back, God was very much at work in the midst of this impossible situation. He was breaking my self-reliance and forming me as a leader that He could work with. He was simultaneously setting the scene for His glory.

If you have found yourself relying on your strengths as a communicator, administrator, relationship-builder, fundraiser or whatever, know that you will one day hit a wall. For those of you who have already hit your wall of inadequacy, you are at a good place. Be grateful for your five loaves and two fish—they are not enough. Know that God shines in the light of our inadequacy.

You are indeed *unequipped* for the work He has chosen for you. Lay your strengths and weaknesses at His feet, depending completely on Him, and you will never be the same. This is Leadership101. This is what Jesus began forming in His team that no human wisdom could ever come up with.

Thoughts for Reflection

- *What situations have you faced lately in which you felt void of resources, whether tangible or intangible?*

- *Have you hit your wall of inadequacy?*

- *Is there a certain wall you keep hitting time after time?*

- *When you have things going right in one area of your leadership, are you finding your shortcomings in another?*

It's time to embrace your inadequacy.

Give your inadequacy to Jesus right now, just as the disciples did when they brought the five loaves and two fish to Him.

As Jesus thanked God for insufficient food before He blessed it, thank God for the inadequacy He has given you.

Acknowledge to Him that you are unable to do what He has called you to do and that only He can do it as He works through you.

Ask God to form you into a leader that is fully dependent on Him.

Note: This wall that you are facing is not a one-time challenge. It is a lifetime reality. Ask Him to help you become the kind of leader who will do what you cannot do with what you do not have for the rest of your life. Ask Him to never let you forget that your inadequacy is not the stopping point for your leadership, it is the starting point for His impact.

CHAPTER 4

HE'S GOT THIS

"Not that we are adequate in ourselves...but our adequacy is from God." (2 Corinthians 3:5)

What a day! Nothing like a God-sized encounter to capture one's attention. The disciples witnessed the feeding of 5,000 from a bag of scraps. No one had ever seen anything like it. They would never forget how Jesus miraculously fed an entire crowd with food to spare. He multiplied their meager resources with His power. Having seen this, surely they were ready for whatever would come their way.

However, the day was not quite over, and Jesus wasn't finished with His teaching. He was about to perform another miracle that would drive home the next reality He was building into the heart of His church.

Lecture This Afternoon, Exam Tonight

It was shortly before evening. The crowd had been fed and could hardly wait to hear more from Jesus. Unexpectedly, Jesus approached His disciples. He made them get into a boat and told them to go across the Sea of Galilee to Bethsaida. He then proceeded to send the crowd away and went up on the mountain to pray (see Mark

6:45-47). The day ended abruptly with the disciples rowing on the sea and Jesus praying on the mountain. It was the calm before the storm—literally.

This storm was not just an ordinary storm; it was a storm that carried the boat way off course, far out into the middle of the Galilee. The fishermen among them were experienced. They had been in many storms on the Sea of Galilee, which was famous for its fierce gales that tossed boats around like little chips of wood and threatened to send them to the bottom. Storms on the Galilee were so intense that when the winds hit and the waves were so high the locals thought the lake was inhabited by demons.

Jesus saw them straining at the oars against the wind, blown way off course, helpless in an insurmountable gale. How could they row when the water was whipped into waves so big they could not control the boat? All they could do was hang on and hope against all hope that they would make it out alive.

By now it was three o'clock in the morning. Jesus waited until they were utterly hopeless and came walking to them on the waves (see Mark 6:48). Why did He wait so long? Did He enjoy seeing them struggle? Not at all. This was no ordinary boat rescue.

Jesus is a teacher at His very core. He wanted to confirm with them that night what He had taught them that afternoon. He's not a mid-semester and finals teacher; He is a learn-it-now and test-immediately teacher. He was delivering a pop-quiz and setting up His next lesson.

Expect the Unexpected

The disciples had no idea that Jesus would deliver them from their dilemma. How could they? No one could row a boat in that storm, and who would ever expect Him to come to them walking on water? They were on their own, and their boat was doomed to sink. Undoubtedly, they expected to die.

Then Jesus did the unexpected. He came to them and did what they could never do: He stilled the storm. Jesus introduced a new way of life to them, a life full of supernatural demands in which they would learn to expect the unexpected as they trusted Him to do what they were powerless to do.

Mark tells us that when He walked to them on the water He intended to pass them by. Why wouldn't He come, still the storm and get in the boat with them? Why did the Lord have to walk on water at all when He could have stilled the storm from the mountain and kept on praying?

The answer lies in an understanding of the term "pass by" in the Old Testament (see Exodus 34:6 [NASB] and 1 Kings 19:11). We read that God "passed by" both Moses and Elijah for one reason: to show them His glory, to make Himself known to them, so He could build confidence in them and work through them as they became His kind of leaders.

This was Jesus' purpose for His disciples as well: He intended to pass them by to show them His glory in the storm. Why? So they could have confidence that He would meet their needs in the most difficult circumstances possible. He wanted them to realize there would be storms in their future far worse than the one they had just encountered.

That afternoon they had learned a significant reality: You must do what you cannot do with what you do not have for the rest of your life. And within just a matter of hours, they learned the second core principle...

Principle #2:
The Reality of Christ's Adequacy

Jesus can do what you cannot do for the rest of your life.

Because Jesus Could

Jesus very deliberately calmed the sea so His disciples would recognize their inadequacy, contrasted with His divine adequacy. He works today just as He did in Galilee, and this miracle still serves as a model of what leadership is like. None of us will ever have enough to do what the Lord calls us to do, but when we obey, He is there with His abundance.

This is the second reality of the altared heart: *Jesus can do what you cannot do for the rest of your life.*

The disciples never had enough resources to do what the Lord commanded; yet when they placed what they had in His hands, they always accomplished His purposes with more than enough left over. The most unlikely group of men imaginable penetrated the Roman Empire with the proclamation of a crucified carpenter who displaced Caesar as Lord.

Our Lord wants to reveal His glory to us also by having us get out of the boat and walk on water in the midst of life's most overwhelming storms. Are we willing to trust Him for that?

We need to know what resources we do have—that's why He told His men to go and find out before they fed the 5,000. Once we know what we have, we will know what we need and realize how desperately dependent we are on Him.

We must bring what little we have to Him and place it in His hands, then wait for His powerful hands to work through our powerless hands to do what He commands. Just as the disciples had more than enough left over, so we will have more than enough to do what

He desires. We will never have enough to do what the Lord commands; but when we obey, He pours out His abundance.

The only way we can have confidence in Jesus is to lose all confidence in ourselves

> **While it is true that without Christ we can do nothing, it is equally true we can do everything He wants us to do through Him.**

and find a new level of trust in Him. Through this radically different kind of confidence, we too can be certain that Christ will work His adequacy through us no matter what we face, whether it's a supernatural task or an overwhelming storm. While it is true that without Christ we can do nothing, it is equally true we can do everything He wants us to do through Him.

He enables us to produce His fruit on the branches of our lives— eternal fruit that He bears through us. One thing we can know for sure: Without Him we can do nothing that has any eternal significance.

That is what I learned as a young pastor stuck in an impossible situation.

Embracing Dependence

When our team at South Hills Community Church discovered in 1977 that we were $100,000 short of erecting our building, we learned in a deeper way than ever to embrace our dependence on the Lord. We could never feed the 5,000—we were overwhelmed and over our heads—but God had already begun to work in me earlier that week, even before I knew of our need.

A few days before our elders' retreat, the Lord had strongly convicted me about staying at South Hills. So when our chairman told us of our need and his fear that the church had given all it could, I remembered that commitment and thought about all that the Lord had done through us from the time we began until then.

I thought of the marriages He had saved through us, the people He had delivered from dire illness through our prayers, the painful moments of discipline we were forced to enact, the non-believers who had come to Christ, our many interns and the people we had sent all over the world for the Gospel, the innumerable counseling sessions the elders and the staff had conducted, the multitude of hospital visits we had made, our care for the poor and the grieving we had comforted. He had done what we could not do.

As I considered this and more, it became evident to me that the Lord had challenged me earlier in the week to recommit to our ministry in order to prepare me to embrace our dependence on Him in an even deeper way.

That's exactly what we did—we fell on our knees and cried out to

God, asking Him to do what we could not do—then we got up off our knees and planned celebration Sunday three weeks later, trusting that God would provide the extra $100,000 we thought we could not possibly raise, and that it would be there.

And it was! Less than three weeks later, the giant earthmovers were creating the pad for our new building, and nine months later we moved in.

Today at the entrance to South Hills stands a pillar of stones, a memorial to what God did when we were at the end of our resources and cried out to Him for His adequacy. South Hills has built two more buildings and recently merged with another church in San Jose as it continues to embrace its dependency on Christ and make a difference for His glory. Jesus did what we could not do, deepening our faith and bringing glory to Himself.

More Than We Can Imagine

Why does Jesus put us in supernatural situations and overwhelming storms so we will have to come face-to-face with ourselves and our limitations? Why is it so important to Jesus that we face our inadequacy? Because He wants to show His greatness through us. He has a task for us we could never dream of. Left to ourselves, many of us would be satisfied to live within the limits of our adequacy: to make a decent living, drive a nice car and have a comfortable home.

Others of us want to stand out more: to make big money, drive a luxury car and own a mansion. Either way, none of us wants to face our inadequacy. We naturally would rather build our kingdom than serve His kingdom—but, as leaders, He won't let us make that choice.

Jesus has far more for us than a career, car and a roof over our heads.

Jesus has far more for us than a career, car and a roof over our heads. He wants us to participate with Him in accomplishing His purposes as He calls us to make an eternal difference through Him. He wants us to be part of His world-changing movement, the movement that has marched through time and across generations until it now blankets the earth. He wants to lift us out of our smallness and into His greatness.

He wants to make us like Himself. None of us is adequate for this.

So Jesus does with us what He did with His disciples that day in Galilee: He brings us to the end of ourselves so He can bring us to the beginning of His power. He focuses on us as He did on His men, singling them out from the crowd, transforming them from spectators into participants by taking what little they had into His hands and then multiplying it through their hands, taking their ordinary bread and turning it into the Bread of Life.

This is why He forces us to focus on our inadequacy by giving us supernatural tasks and putting us into overwhelming storms. **He wants us to partner with Him in His eternal purpose so we share with Him in His ultimate glory.** He wants us to rule with Him over the forces of evil and destruction that distort men and women made in God's image into terrible perversions of themselves. He wants us to restore these human ruins into the glorious temples they were created to be. Why would we want to hide in our puny little kingdoms when we can exalt Him in His eternal kingdom?

The feeding of the 5,000 and walking on water, as great and amazing as they were, were nothing compared to going into all the world and making disciples of every nation, tribe and tongue—yet that is what Jesus was preparing them and us to do, and He had to teach them their inadequacy so He could teach them His adequacy.

The only way He could do that was to immerse them in demands that would drown them if they depended on themselves. He also had to show them what He could do through them, so He involved them in meeting the very needs they could never hope to meet on their own. What He did with His disciples, He does with us.

Embracing Dependence—Again

It was 5 a.m., Sunday, December 20, 2015. A cold, clammy fear in the pit of my stomach forced me out of bed, into my study and drove me to Isaiah in search of comfort and strength. The end of the year was coming, but the money wasn't. It appeared we would not meet our year-end budget.

I admit that 2015 had been a year of struggle for me in several ways. Stress in a relationship I could not resolve had gripped me, bringing me to the brink of depression. It had also been a year of facing my physical limitations. I have health, energy and opportunities, but I also have a birth certificate that reminds me of my age. I wondered, *Will I live long enough to complete my commitments?* And now the year-end loomed.

I faced supernatural challenges and could not resolve the tension in my life no matter how hard I tried. I could not change my mortality no matter how meticulously I took care of myself. I could not write a check to meet the financial need no matter how much I desired.

I had to feed the 5,000, but all I had was five loaves and two fish—and I wasn't sure I even had that much. So I did what Jesus told the disciples to do once they knew what they had: "Bring them here to Me" (Matthew 14:18). I brought my five loaves and two fish to Jesus in prayer and turned to Isaiah 41:9-10: "Do not fear for I am with you."

I released the relationship tension to God. Then I decided my mortality is God's business, not mine, and I told Him I would continue doing what I've been doing until He stops me. Finally, I gave our income to

Him while I announced the need to our constituency and looked to Him to multiply what we had so that we would be able to meet our year-end commitment and feed 5,000. With that I had immediate, confident peace.

We experienced Christ's adequacy, although not by December 31. When we were short of our budget on the last day of December, I still *knew* He would provide. Imagine our excitement when a large check arrived January 15, slowed up by the post office but postmarked December 31, 2015. And imagine our even greater delight when we learned three months later— yes, three months—that another check had been sent at the end of the year but had gone to the wrong address. It would *exactly* complete our year-end need.

> **Leadership in His name is a matter of radical dependence upon Christ, and He alone has the power to make a leader fruitful.**

Even after our deadline, our faithful God provided and showed me I had no reason to fear. God's timing is not always the same as ours, but it is always perfect. Once again, I had come back to the altar and to Jesus' first two realities—the ones he had reaffirmed over and over in my life:

You must do what you cannot do with what you do not have;

and

Jesus can do what you cannot do for the rest of your life.

All leaders fail. God deliberately brings leaders into places of failure to show us two things: our inadequacy and His adequacy. Even the most skillful leader will produce no enduring fruit without Christ's enablement. And adding more skill will not suffice. Leadership in His name is a matter of radical dependence upon Christ, and He alone has the power to make a leader fruitful.

We can know this truth in our heads, but it makes no difference to our hands—in what we do—until it impacts our hearts. When we live empowered by this reality, we begin to bear fruit as God works through us.

Thoughts for Reflection

- *What storms are raging in your life as a leader?*

- *What challenges are you are struggling with that you simply do not want to face?*

- *What things in your life does God want you to do that you are close to giving up on?*

- *Is it possible that God designed you to be insufficient in your own strength for the task He has given you?*

- *What keeps you from trusting God to do what He wants you to do? Be specific in your answers, especially about those areas where you don't want to give up control and trust God.*

It's time to embrace His adequacy.

Decide now that you will embrace a new level of dependence on Christ by praying this prayer: "Lord, I give up! I have tried to be in control of my life, but I can't do it. The life you have called me to live is bigger than I am, and I don't know what to do. Please, Lord, take over and do whatever you want."

Trust Him as you wait for His adequacy to work through you.

CHAPTER 5

IT'S HARDER THAN YOU THINK

"For they considered not the miracle of the loaves: for their hearts were hardened." (Mark 6:52)

The Gospel of Mark provides many examples that illustrate how the disciples thought they understood Jesus. In reality, they didn't have the slightest idea what He was saying—and they didn't even know it. After all the time spent with Jesus while listening to His teaching, they had not gained any understanding. Mark 6:51-52 tells us that the disciples were amazed when Jesus rescued them by calming the storm, and they had not understood the significance of the loaves.

Where was the disconnect? How is it that they had heard the lecture but failed the exam? What kept them from serving God with purity and wholeness—and stands as a barrier to leaders today?

Jesus was dealing head-on with the issue of man—the issue that plagued the leaders of old—the issue that thwarted the likes of David and Solomon. The reason they failed the exam? Their hardened hearts.

Setting the Stage

After Jesus feeds the 5,000 and calms the storm, He continues teaching and demonstrating His adequacy and authority. In fact, Mark 7-8 describes a lot of activity.

First, there's a confrontation between Him and the Pharisees concerning external washings. When the Pharisees and scribes ask Jesus why His disciples ate with impure hands, He responds,

> *"Rightly did Isaiah prophesy of you hypocrites, as it is written:*
>
> > *'This people honors me with their lips,*
> > *but their heart is far from me.*
> > *'but in vein do they worship me,*
> > *teaching as doctrines the precepts of men.'" (7:6-7)*

When the heart is not pure, it affects all of life.

This was followed by a conversation Jesus had with His disciples in which they asked Him what He meant when He spoke about the heart. Jesus' answer was to the point: It is not what's on the outside but what's in the heart that defiles a person and determines purity. When the heart is not pure, it affects all of life (see Mark 7:1-23).

And this takes us to our next reality of altared leadership...

Principle #3:
The Reality of the Hardened Heart

Your heart is the heart of the matter.

You see, the Jesus way is all about the heart—always has been, always will be.

Four Miracles, One Message

Next, Mark lays out a series of four key miracles. As you read them, you will see that God was setting them up for an explosive question that Jesus would ask His disciples—and it is one leaders need to ask daily.

The first miracle involves a Syrophonecian woman in Tyre (see Mark 7:24-30) who came to Jesus in faith, even though she had little knowledge of Messiah. A Gentile, this woman had heard of Jesus and learned that He cast out demons. She acted on her limited understanding and begged Him to deliver her young daughter from a demon.

Jesus marveled at her faith. This woman had almost no knowledge, yet she trusted the Lord to do what she could not do. The disciples, on the other hand, had gained great knowledge concerning Messiah—but in many ways they had gleaned little insight from their time with Him.

Imagine how this struck the disciples. She had just passed the test they had failed, and Jesus applauded her publicly. At the same time, Jesus' message to the twelve was clear: *Your time with me has not penetrated your hardened hearts; therefore, your minds have been darkened.*

Next, Jesus moved with his men to a village where some people brought a deaf man who could hardly speak (see Mark 7:32-37). He opened the man's ears and loosened his tongue. He was making His second point with them about their hearts—He was teaching them one core message concerning the cross: *You are not hearing Me, so you are not getting my point. Your hardened hearts have deafened your ears, and you are not able to speak clearly.*

All good teachers use repetition to reinforce a vital point and make it even stronger. This is exactly what Jesus did with the next miracle of feeding of 4,000 with seven loaves, a similar but different incident from the feeding of the 5,000 (see Mark 8:1-10).

What was His point in repeating this miracle? Jesus was saying, "I mean it, men; you have to understand this. You must do what you cannot do, but I will do what I can do through you." In other words, a hardened heart would paralyze their hands and prevent them from doing what He was calling them to do.

A lot more was happening than was sinking in. It was evident the disciples were not quite getting it...

Back in the boat, the disciples were locked in a meaningless debate because they had only brought one loaf of bread. Jesus was incredulous. How could they be talking about bread when He was speaking to them about their hearts? They had observed the miracles but had totally missed the point.

Now comes Jesus' explosive question in Mark 8:17:

"Do you have hardened hearts?"

These five words must have stung. After all, the disciples were chosen by Jesus. They had spent considerable time with Him. What did their Leader mean by "hardened heart"? And if Jesus asked it of these men, how could it not be the ultimate question for all of us?

Interestingly, Mark referenced the disciples' hardened hearts after Jesus calmed the storm: "Then He got into the boat with them, and the wind stopped; and they were utterly astonished, for they had not gained any insight from the incident of the loaves, but their hearts were hardened" (Mark 6:51-52).

How could Mark say this about men who had sacrificed their family life, financial security and cultural acceptability? It is certainly a harsh judgment of those Jesus had personally called, trained and sent out to minister, those who would ultimately die for Him.

Mark asserts this claim with no explanation at all. And the fact is, the disciples did have hardened hearts—Jesus said so.

Finally, we come to the fourth miracle, the two-stage healing of the blind man (Mark 8:22-26). The message to the disciples is key: *You are halfway there, but you mix truth with trees. Your hardened hearts are keeping you from understanding truth clearly, and this causes you to miss the point about Me. There is a mist over your eyes; and although you are being healed, you are not nearly as far along as you think. I must turn your trees into truth, or I won't be able to use you.*

A hardened heart refers to a stubborn, willful, unteachable heart that learns without perceiving, listens without hearing, looks without seeing and acts without impacting. It deafens the ears, blinds the eyes, darkens the mind and paralyzes the hands. It says the right thing but misses the real point because it relies on itself to do what only Jesus can do.

Each of the four miracles points to one central theme: Your hearts are hardened, and they impact you in every way. Do you not understand (as the Gentile woman did)? Do you have eyes to see and ears to hear (as the deaf man did)? How many leftovers did you have following the two feedings (I freed your hands to serve)? Are you blind to the truth (you mix truth with trees)?

The Gospel of Mark makes this reality clear as we see how Jesus formed His men into the kind of leaders He would commission to carry out His mission on earth. We see Jesus wrestle with the hearts of His men, and we realize His greatest concern was neither their knowledge nor their skills but their hearts.

Over the years, I've learned that heart struggles can darken the mind and paralyze the hands of leaders—and almost no one is exempt. As a result, we end up mired in our inadequacy, striving vainly to feed the 5,000 and ride out the storm.

> **We see Jesus wrestle with the hearts of His men, and we realize His greatest concern was neither their knowledge nor their skills but their hearts.**

Common Ground

Years ago, I was part of a team at Dallas Theological Seminary that developed an assessment process called LEAD (Leadership Evaluation And Development). This five-day assessment was designed to serve four leaders at a time (along with their spouse if they were married) and methodically moved them through a set of modules led by expert and experienced coaches.

All participants had to fill out an assessment form of 50-75 pages per couple in response to some penetrating questions the coaches received and reviewed beforehand. The assessment focused on three areas of a leader's life: the growing-up period and their marriage and family; the leader's life dream as discerned through God's guiding hand revealed by their life story; and the leader's current ministry fit.

I coached over 400 LEAD participants and discovered the same pattern in virtually all of them: They all were impacted by heart struggles. There were varying degrees of impact, but there seemed to be no exceptions.

My view of leadership was transformed by hours of intense conversation with these leaders from around the globe who desired an altared heart that would make them altered leaders, but who struggled with some of the same issues that Jesus had to confront in His disciples.

One of the most important changes in my thinking is this: Facing our inadequacy and finding Christ's adequacy is much more demanding than we realize because nothing in our experience or education has prepared us to do what Jesus wants us to do.

I had always thought leadership was about getting things done. It consisted of directing people, setting goals, accomplishing vision

I had always thought leadership was about getting things done.

and striving to lead in ways that were best for God—and the leader. I had no idea how much the hidden issues of the heart control the leader's head and hands so that the leader is at the mercy of his or her struggles, whether it be anger, pride, fear, unhealthy competition or a myriad of other responses to life.

The heart must be changed, but that happens only when we face what is in our hearts and realize that they are centers of control and self-protection.

Who, Me?

If the disciples' hearts were hardened, and they walked with Jesus, how likely are ours to be hardened as well?

As leaders, many of us live in denial of our hardened hearts. We do this because we don't know what else to do. The emptiness inside of us, our fears, the struggles we sense but can't identify are so great we don't know what else to do but to deny our feelings.

Let's look at some of the characteristics of the hardened heart that we share with the disciples:

- When we face overwhelming situations (like feeding the 5,000), we ask the Lord to remove the problem because we think we lack the resources to meet the need just as they did.

- We protect ourselves from risk and seek to control life even though God wants us to release control and turn in desperate dependence to Him.

- On our ministry teams we do exactly what the disciples did: We compete to be the greatest, we strive for the highest positions, we are invulnerable and ambitious and we become defensive and self-protective when corrected.

- We struggle with sin (see Romans 7:14-25) and wrestle with the flesh, fulfilling its desires on a regular basis, bringing on dissensions and divisions.

- We grieve the Holy Spirit by disobeying biblical commands, which results in anger, malice, desires for vindication and vengeance.

We are so much like the disciples that we must have hardened hearts. What else can explain our responses?

Even though we have the Holy Spirit and a new heart, our old responses continue in us, and we often act as if we're not new at all. Many times we presume leadership is the fruit of our hands—

meaning our abilities and strengths—but for Jesus, leadership is the fruit of our hearts.

Mark's aim was to show his readers that Jesus is the Son of God who came with a purpose—not only to die for us, but also to live through us producing heart transformation. He is looking for a worldwide, unstoppable movement carried out *through* inadequate men and women called to make His power known through their weakness.

This is the wonder of our call, and only our hardened hearts can stop us. When our hearts are not pure, every dimension of our leadership is affected.

Running the Race

No one understood the process of heart transformation better than Paul. A bright light, a fallen man, a convicting voice, blinded eyes—what a conversion event that was. However, Paul soon realized that the event was just the beginning of a process that would take his whole life. He knew the process was costly, that it mattered and that it was never finished until he reached the prize he strained for so mightily and entered into Christ's presence.

The process cost him everything he valued: his history, his significance, even his identity—it all became waste in his mind because it hindered his freedom to reach the prize (see Philippians 3:1-6). The process also mattered because he knew he could fall short and be disqualified from the race (see 1 Corinthians 9:27).

Most of all, he wanted to reach the prize that the process promised: to achieve the high calling of God in Christ Jesus, to finish the race well, to thunder down the home stretch to the cheers of all who ran before him right into the arms of Jesus—the ultimate Prize (see Philippians 3:7-14).

Paul knew, though, that he had not yet attained the prize even though he had been under unjust Roman arrest for four years while he went hungry and his fellow believers undermined him (see Philippians 1:12-18). He who wrote "old things have passed away; new things have come" (2 Corinthians 5:17) knew that the old does not give up without a struggle, and the new comes only over time.

We, too, are in that same race, reaching for that same prize. Yet a barrier is blocking that prize, demanding a daily choice to draw on Christ's power to feed the 5,000. It is our hardened hearts, the barrier that must be progressively broken as we strive for our prize in the high calling of God in Christ Jesus. It is only as we enter into brokenness that our leadership can become whole.

A Process, Not an Event

Our decision to trust Christ was an event. Our determination to follow Christ was an event. Our decision to live in fellowship with

Christ was an event. But each of these events introduced a process of growth that will take us deeper and deeper into Christ and into ourselves than we have ever gone. Each process involves cycles of confusion, struggle, failure, epiphany, joy

We must stop looking for quick fixes.

and deliverance in Christ—and this happens over and over again as long as we live.

Placing our heart on Christ's altar and taking up the cross is *not* an event. It is not something that we did only when we were children or in junior high.

It is a lifetime process of returning to the altar again and again, each time releasing more and more of our heart to God and allowing Him to transform us in new ways. This means there is no switch that will turn off the fears and drives of our hardened hearts. There is no switch that will make these struggles go away and make us into perfectly sanctified, totally dependent followers of Christ. That is why the biblical writers never gave us steps to solve our problems.

Instead, they called us to a relationship with Jesus that requires us to depend on His adequacy, to release all to Him as He calls us to place our hearts on His altar and enter into the process of growing by trusting Him.

We must stop looking for quick fixes. *Only then will we enter into the hard work of growing Christ's way.*

Thoughts for Reflection

- *Do you have a hardened heart? Let the same Jesus who asked this question of the disciples examine you with it.*

- *In what ways does your hardened heart tend to surface? Be specific in your responses.*

- *In what areas of your life are you walking in disobedience to scripture? Are you willing to be vulnerable before God, confess these areas and experience His cleansing?*

- *In what ways is your hardened heart affecting those around you?*

You will never see God's will for your life come to pass outside of a pure and pliable heart. It is time to come clean. Confess to Him that your heart is hard and in need of His touch. Determine to draw on Christ's adequacy to grow consistently in overcoming your hardened heart.

CHAPTER 6

THE WRONG GAUGES

"Get behind me, Satan; for you are not setting your mind on God's interests, but man's." (Jesus to Peter, Mark 8:33)

So far, the curriculum for world-change that Jesus has been delivering to the disciples has been a profound ride: miracles, more miracles, provoking questions and the analysis of the heart. All in all, this was not your typical leadership course.

At this point, the way Jesus was working to shape them was reaching a pivotal moment. It was, in effect, time for the midterm exam. As exams go, it was quite simple—only one question.

Jesus was notorious for starting conversations with a question. After He had been teaching His disciples for almost three years, He posed a very straightforward question that led to a dramatic exchange between Him and one of His most outspoken disciples. The question is significant for us today, and the answer we give determines everything about our life and our leadership.

An Unforeseen Plot Twist

One day Jesus was walking with His disciples in the area of Caesarea Philippi, north of Galilee. He asked them: "Who do people say that the Son of Man is?" (Matthew 16:13). The disciples apparently had heard comparisons and mentioned spiritual giants including John the Baptist, Elijah, Jeremiah and "one of the prophets."

It's not that these were ridiculous answers—they were all men of God. But that's just the point: They were mere men, not deity. For people to see Jesus as just another religious person shows that they didn't truly recognize Jesus as the Messiah, the Savior of the world.

Then Jesus turned the question to the disciples. In a sense, it was a test. "But who do you say that I am?" He asked (16:15).

It's such a simple question that it's easy to gloss over it. But this is a powerful question and still deeply relevant for us today.

Peter stepped up to the plate and identified Jesus as the Christ. Jesus blessed him for his response (see Matthew 16:16-17). The fact is, Peter had rightly identified Jesus as the Christ, but Jesus realized there was still much more He needed to communicate about Himself. It was time to expand their understanding.

As background, the "Son of Man" was a familiar phrase. When Jesus posed the first question, it likely didn't catch the disciples off-guard. They would have remembered it from their study of the Scriptures.

In Daniel 7:14, Daniel describes his vision of the Son of Man as He approached the Ancient of Days, where He received authority, glory and power. That title, "Son of Man," spoke volumes to the ancient followers of Jesus, the men He was forming to lead His cause.

They were confident that Jesus, the Messiah, would overthrow Rome and establish His kingdom here on earth. As His followers, they believed Jesus was going to share His power with them. Over and over in their heads they had pictured their pending royalty. "Fit us for a crown!" was their expectation and their cry.

Then Jesus spoke a little word with a very big meaning: *must*, the strongest word of necessity in the New Testament (see Mark 8:31). His disciples had to be filled with anticipation: It would happen because it *must* happen—His dominion would be everlasting, and His kingdom would never be destroyed.

Jesus was asserting that He was the Messiah, the Son of Man, the one who must overthrow Rome and exalt Israel; and they, His faithful believers who have been with Him since the beginning, were starting to envision their soon-to-be glamorous lives as rulers with Him!

Suffer?

The next part of the conversation must have confused them greatly. Jesus used the shocking word "suffer" (16:21). Where was suffering in Daniel 7? What was Jesus talking about? It sounded like He was talking about a cross, not a crown. How could that be?

The Messiah doesn't die; no, the Messiah is supposed to overthrow Rome. If Messiah dies, there are no crowns for anyone.

Jesus was speaking painfully clear about the cross to come. There were no puzzling parables, no mysteries of the kingdom, nothing to guess about. As impossible as it was for their minds to grasp, Jesus was going to die. Such clarity brought a strong reaction, an almost volatile response.

Peter faced a cross/crown decision at that moment. He was thrown by the thought that his ticket to power could slip away. He made his choice instantly. As soon as Jesus spoke these words, Peter was propelled to his feet as he made his choice: Crown, of course!

We are told that Peter took Jesus aside (Mark 8:32). Somehow, he moved Jesus physically, whether he put his arm around His shoulder or took Him by the arm, and rebuked Him.

Think of it, the Messiah being manhandled by one of His followers. Peter reacted with great firmness and used the strongest words available to him: "God forbid it, Lord! This shall never happen to You" (Matthew 16:22).

Jesus Responds

When Jesus turned around to see His disciples, He knew they were thinking exactly the same thing Peter was. He could not let Peter's rebuke stand without a response in kind—a strong rebuke for His key leader.

"Get behind me, Satan!" (Mark 8:33). In other words, Jesus was saying, "Get in line where you belong: following Me, not leading Me; submitting to Me, not controlling me; learning from Me, not thinking like Satan."

But why did Jesus call Peter Satan? It was not that Peter had suddenly become demonic or was controlled by Satan, but that Peter had revealed his true heart and motives.

> **A crown without a cross was Satan's appeal to Jesus and the dream of many leaders.**

Truly, the idea of the cross was so totally foreign to Peter that he thought like Satan. After all, taking up a crown without the cross represents the very heart of Satan and was exactly what he had tempted Jesus to do in the wilderness (Matthew 4:1-11). A crown without a cross was Satan's appeal to Jesus and the dream of many leaders.

Then Jesus confronted Peter with some of the most insightful words any leader could hear as He cut right to the core of Peter's hardened heart, revealing his misfocused mind:

"You are not setting your mind on God's interests, but man's" (Mark 8:33).

What penetrating words—words that are just as true today as they were when Jesus uttered them. No words have helped me understand myself and my mixed drives better than these. Remember, Jesus said these words to a man who had given up everything to follow Him.

Many Christian leaders today are actually crown seekers to one extent or another. When our hearts are hardened and we want control to pursue our own interests in Jesus' name, we are headed down a path of destruction.

This brings us to our next reality...

Principle #4:
The Reality of the Misfocused Mind

The hardened heart misfocuses the leader's mind.

As hard as it sounds, even the most glorious of "Christian" endeavors can subversively find their foundation in the pursuit of building our kingdoms over His.

Our Pursuit

Ambition is the single biggest issue among leaders in the body of Christ, the greatest mark of broken leadership among us. When we think we have crowns coming to us, we act in ways to get and keep those crowns.

Yes, we're committed to Christ and serving Him—but we still want a crown. We want to hold on to our power and live life on our terms. Our misfocused minds cause us to seek the interests of man rather than the interests of God. We need God's power to free us from our power—and only the cross can do that.

> **We need God's power to free us from our power—and only the cross can do that.**

Peter's insight was absolutely right: Jesus is the Christ, the Son of the Living God—and that is why Christ's reference to the cross was such a shock to him. His mind was misfocused because his heart was hardened and He had missed the truth of this prophecy.

Because his thinking was centered on a crown and not a cross, Peter could not fathom that Jesus came to take up the cross, not to distribute crowns. He was reaching for a crown, and Jesus was handing him a cross. As he reached for power, Jesus was calling him to weakness.

It's Completely Natural

It was completely natural for Peter to think the way he did because he had prophecy on his side from many passages of the Old Testament. All of those promises said the same thing in different ways: God would send his Anointed One to establish His kingdom on earth.

Peter felt sure that he was right and became threatened by our Lord's words. It is what drove him to rebuke the Son of God. What Peter, the disciples and all of ancient Israel had missed was Isaiah 53, where we see that the Lord would be a suffering servant.

Peter was absolutely convinced that Jesus was the Messiah, and this filled him with the expectation of a kingdom and a crown in this world. He knew that if Jesus went to the cross, there would be no throne. Jesus simply asserted God's will and called for Peter to submit to it; but because his mind was misfocused, Peter could not accept what Jesus was saying. Although radically committed to Christ, he had a hardened heart.

Been There

I've been there. Have you? Since the time I was a child, I have been radically committed to Christ. At the same time, I have found myself driven to achieve success on man's terms, striving for recognition, driven to seek man's interests. My heart was open to God yet hardened by self. I have lived with a misfocused mind that drove me to pursue man's interests rather than God's.

Yet our Lord's words ("You are not setting your mind on God's interests, but man's") rang true in my heart when I first discovered them. They made me realize that I have had the same drives as Peter. The interests of man have been marbled through my deep motives to serve Christ, as I have had expectations of significance because of my commitment to Him—success according to man's terms, all mixed in with my true desire to glorify Him.

It was painful for me to realize this, even as it had to be painful for Peter to hear what Jesus said to him, but these words brought deep insight to me and have given me some of the greatest freedom in my life.

These words also helped me to begin to understand what the wall of inadequacy is all about; I finally realized that I could never escape that wall. I could not avoid the innate limitations and flaws deep inside me. In that moment, I also knew the true depth of my utter dependency on Christ, my only hope of glory—but His glory and not mine.

Secular Gauges on a Spiritual Flight

Somewhere along the way, many of us as leaders buy into the lie that "Christian" or even ministry success can be defined on our own terms or by the markings of secular success. Think about it. How common is it to define your leadership success in quantitative terms? Or to compare your results with others'?

Is it possible that we are using cultural gauges to measure our biblical effectiveness in leadership?

Could we be using secular gauges on a spiritual flight?

When we measure ourselves by the interests of man, we are using the wrong gauges—the secular gauges of position, power, fame, recognition, influence—but we are on a spiritual flight. You can see the wrong gauges everywhere in leaders who maneuver themselves into positions of power so they can be successful, and then take control to protect their interests and maintain their control.

Is it any wonder we often find ourselves off course and running smack into walls of inadequacy?

Let's face it, left to ourselves, man is inherently driven toward power, success and control—and as leaders we are not exceptions. Until we submit our interests to Christ's will, we will serve ourselves and not Him, no matter what we think or say.

To lead God's way, we must turn from doing our will in Jesus' name as we go from power to humility, success to service and control to sacrifice.

We have to recognize our own temptation to allow our minds to be misfocused, thinking that we are pursuing God's interests when we actually are pursuing our own desires. Current leadership thinking fans our desire for man's interest in the name of Jesus. The only way to get back on course on our spiritual flight is through the experience of taking up the cross.

Unrealistic Expectations

Consider the internal process Peter went through in deciding to rebuke Jesus. He had established knowledge: Jesus is the Christ, and the Christ was to come, overthrow Rome and establish the promised kingdom. This established knowledge created expectations in Peter, and his expectations defined his identity as a follower of Jesus. He expected a crown.

We follow the same process and enter into the same struggles as Peter. Even though we are not always aware of this, our expectations not only define our identity but also define what we think is God's will for us. As a result, we feel He is unfaithful when He doesn't meet our anticipations.

An expectation is a demand we make of the Lord and others that *must* be fulfilled. Frequently, our expectations are deeply ingrained in our identity, so we feel vulnerable and violated when we don't get what we think is coming to us—what we see as our right.

Expectations can grow out of our understanding of God's promises, our concept of God's faithfulness and our perspective of reality based on what we think God should do. Yet often our expectations grow out of a misunderstanding of God's promises or timing, just as Peter's did.

Think about the following list of expectations many of us as Christians may have. All of these show that, at heart, we are driven by man's interests, human values and not God's. Can you identify with any of these expectations?

- I will be successful, as I measure it, because I am obeying Jesus.

- My accomplishments make me somebody.

- Jesus owes me because I've given up so much for Him.

- My followers should work to make me successful.

- God will give me a spouse.

- My spouse should understand me.

- Because I waited to marry a Christian, my marriage will be tension-free.

- I can expect my spouse to understand the demands I face and never be stressed by them.

- I can expect my spouse to cover for me with our children.

- My children will never suffer.

- My children will make me look good in the Christian community.

- Because I am following Jesus, I will have no financial concerns.

- Life will be fair—no one will ever mistreat me.

- I will be valued for every contribution I make.

- I will be free from illness.

All of these expectations are about control, not trust. We want what we want when we want it, and we don't want to pass through hard struggles and trust the Lord for what He is doing in our lives.

...when we focus our minds on the interests of God, we can trust Him to be our security, no matter what we face.

We want the struggles to go away, like the disciples wanted the 5,000 to go away rather than trust Jesus to meet the need. What we really want is to have life on our terms. However, God cannot give us life on our terms; but when we focus our minds on the interests of God, we can trust Him to be our security, no matter what we face.

As you may have discovered, we cannot possibly control life. When we try to, we become fearful and angry, and life begins to control us—to the point we are completely out of control. All who set their minds on God's interest and not man's will trust God for His control, His purpose and His expectations for us.

How can we be delivered from pursuing man's interests in the name of Jesus? Only by having our hearts transformed. Until we are ready for this transformation, we will resist God even as Peter did.

No matter what expectations and biblical support Peter—and we—think we have, the cross redefines our expectations because the cross redefines our reality. It is the cross that breaks us so we can exercise altared leadership.

Embracing a New Mind

The first time I embraced God's altar, I was 12 years old and meant it. Since then, I have discovered that the older I get, the greater God's demands become.

The day I was unexpectedly informed that I was being moved from a position I loved to one I liked at best, I faced a new call to the altared heart. It was a call to obey without anger or vindication. It was death—again.

I had a choice: Would I enter into the reality of the altared heart in a deeper way than ever before, or would I resent an assignment I could not control and didn't want?

After great struggle over an extended period of time, I finally told God, "It's all in the grave. Raise what you will."

The reason I didn't like God's will for me was that it wasn't turning out the way I expected it to. My expectations were not being met, yet I discovered later that God was doing far more through me than I could ever have expected.

What Are You Pursuing?

Do you ever join Peter in rebuking Jesus for God's will for you—for the cross in your life? Do you ever complain to God about how your leadership opportunity is turning out? Do you feel that you gave up your own desires to follow His and now He's letting you down somehow?

If your mind is misfocused due to a hardened heart, you are pursuing your crown rather than Christ's cross. Taking up the cross in a fresh way will free you from the discontentment of your expectations.

God has no interest in man's interests. To lead God's way, we must turn from doing our will in Jesus' name. *We need God's power to free us from our power*, and the cross is the source of His power.

Thoughts for Reflection

Review the list of expectations in this chapter and identify those that are not being met in ways you think they should be.

- *What additional frustrations would you add to this list?*

- *In what ways are they not being met?*

- *How does this make you feel? Write down your feelings about this disappointment. What does this reveal about you that you never saw before?*

- *Is the will of God good enough for you?*

- *What has God done in your life that is far better than you could ever have expected?*

- *Sometimes we are so focused on what we want that we fail to see the great things that God is doing in our lives. Could this be happening to you?*

- *How would your attitude change if you thanked God for not giving you what you expected? Right now, thank Him for His limitations in your life.*

CHAPTER 7

THE OVERLOOKED POWER

"...If anyone wishes to come after Me, he must deny himself, and take up his cross and follow me." (Jesus to leaders, Mark 8:34)

Think of how Peter must have felt. First, he had been blessed for acknowledging that Jesus was the Messiah; and then moments later, Jesus reprimanded him and called him Satan. These harsh words must have wounded Peter, and Jesus could not leave him in such pain so "He summoned the crowd with His disciples" (Mark 8:34) and issued a call that brought clarity to their misfocused minds—the call of the cross. Once again, Jesus was calling his followers not only to the deepest level of commitment, but to a whole new purpose for life, and heeding this call is imperative for every Christian leader today.

The Only Power That Can Change Us

As our Lord was forming His disciples for ministry, He had identified two barriers between their inadequacy and His adequacy: their hardened hearts and their misfocused minds. We discussed in the last chapter that the disciples thought for sure God would send His Anointed One to establish His kingdom on earth. When Jesus told the disciples that "the Son of Man must suffer many things and be rejected by the elders and the chief priests and the scribes, and be killed" (Mark 8:31), it jolted them completely.

After rebuking Peter for not setting His mind "on God's interests but on man's," Jesus delivered a clarion call for the ages:

> **"...If anyone wishes to come after Me, he must deny himself, and take up his cross and follow Me" (8:34).**

Through this passionate plea, Jesus was saying that only the cross can deliver us from hardened hearts and misfocused minds.

Without taking up the cross and following the Man who carried the cross on His back, we are as powerless as Peter when he so blindly boasted of his own prowess.

By taking up our cross, we lay hold of His powerful grace that delivers us from futile self-dependence to the enablement of Christ-dependence.

This leads to our next reality...

Principle #5:
The Reality of the Forgotten Cross

The hardened heart misfocuses the leader's mind.

Taking up the cross transforms our minds from being crown-focused to becoming cross-bearing.

The cross is the missing element in leadership because we often don't realize that it alone has the power to change a leader's heart. "The message of the cross is the only force that can change the world for the better, and the only force that has actually proved that it can do so," writes Peter Bolt. "It is time for the cross of Christ to be proclaimed once again, loudly and strongly."[4] Unless the cross changes leaders' hearts, the cross can never change the world.

Taking up the cross transforms our minds from being crown-focused to becoming cross-bearing. It means we face God's holiness, confess our sin, accept His mercy and receive His power through His grace. It is a progressive process in which the cross moves deeper and deeper into our hearts, shining the light of its truth into the secret folds of our lives so our minds are refocused and our hands released.

An Identity Transplant

It is interesting that those words "follow Me" were the very words

4. Peter Bolt, *The Cross from A Distance*, InterVarsity Press, 2004, p. 78.

Jesus used when He called Peter on the shore of the Sea of Galilee (Mark 16:17).

Jesus was saying to Peter—and to us, "If you truly meant it the day you chose to come after Me, then you need to give up your old identity and find your new identity in Me. You must deny everything associated with your old self, controlled by sin, and allow Me to refocus your mind and transform your heart so that you become My leader."

We move from being a hardened-heart leader to becoming a cross-broken leader—that's our new identity. If this is what we want, then we must deny our crown-driven self and say "yes" to the cross.

What is this self we must deny? That innate, power-seeking, control-demanding core of our being that screams for the satisfaction and recognition of a crown. We must turn away from all of the selfish ambition, anger, fear, unforgiveness and every other work of the flesh that wars against the Holy Spirit and drives us toward the crown. Only the power of the cross enables this denial.

To do this we must gain our strength in His weakness, in His decision to give up all control and release Himself entirely to His Father no matter what it cost Him. We must follow Him. This means unmasking our puny little glory, releasing our imaginary sovereignty, dying to our futile self and finding our new identity through the cross.

When we lose ourselves in Him, we can find ourselves through Him. This means giving ourselves to Him with nothing held back for whatever He wants. We go where He wants and live as He commands for all our lives, no matter what the cost.

If this is not your passionate desire, you will never be Christ's kind of leader—and you can be sure that the dust of death will cover all you do.

Sooner or later, who we truly are will show through, no matter how we dress ourselves in discipleship verbiage. The tarnish of the crown will dull the fool's gold of our professed commitment.

One of the biggest mistakes the modern church makes is to treat discipleship and leadership as separate disciplines. Often, we reduce discipling to fill-in-the blank workbooks. While these can be useful tools, filling in the blanks never made anyone a disciple.

No assignment in history is more demanding than this, and no task on earth demands leadership more.

Beyond that, Jesus did more than "disciple" his men as we use the term today. At the end of the discipleship process, He gave them the Great Commission, the greatest leadership task in history.

Jesus was forming His men to become the kind of leaders who could transform entire societies with His Good News. No assignment in history is more demanding than this, and no task on earth demands leadership more. Who else seeks to influence every culture on earth to go in a radically different direction more than Christians who carry out the Great Commission?

Cultural vs. Biblical Leadership

Everywhere I go I see a common pattern: Christian leadership that is more cultural than biblical. It doesn't matter what role leaders fill, whether business, ministry, education or another responsibility, the tendency is to follow the culture rather than the Bible.

It is no wonder this is true when you consider the advantages of cultural leadership over biblical leadership:

- Cultural leadership is *powerful*; biblical leadership is *weak*.

- Cultural leadership is *independent*; biblical leadership is *dependent*.

- Cultural leadership is *the way of wisdom* in the world's eyes; biblical leadership is *the way of foolishness* in the world's eyes.

- Cultural leadership *seeks recognition*; biblical leadership *seeks humility*.

- Cultural leadership *dominates its followers*; biblical leadership *serves its followers*.

- Cultural leadership *elevates the leader*; biblical leadership *lowers the leader*.

- Cultural leadership *protects* the leader; biblical leadership *sacrifices* the leader.

- Cultural leadership *conforms* to the culture; biblical leadership *conflicts* with the culture.

- Cultural leadership is about *power, success and control*; biblical leadership is about *service, humility and sacrifice*.

Both cultural and biblical leadership are about love. Cultural leadership **loves and serves self**; biblical leadership **loves and serves others**.

Who wouldn't choose cultural leadership over biblical leadership when you consider all its advantages? But here's the grave disadvantage of cultural leadership: It leads to ***death***.

All cultural leadership results in the death of a project, the death of an empire, the death of the leader, the death of a church.

We can feel this death in our fear, covetousness, competition, selfish ambition, impatience, unforgiveness, resentment and our anger. We can feel it as we strive to hold on to what we have gained and resist others who threaten our position. We know cultural leadership means fading glory, the glory that fades behind our mask of success.

Cultural leadership is all about crowns, but every crown we seek becomes tarnished the moment we touch it, so we continue our constant pursuit of power. Even when we gain the crown we seek, it's full of emptiness.

The Cross and Leadership

Biblical leadership, however, means growing glory. It needs no mask; it is open and confident (see 2 Corinthians 3:7-11). The cross offers us hope, the hope of death that results in life. It's a death unlike anything we have ever known: the death of Christ that raises us to life and gives us the true hope of glory.

As Christ was glorified through the cross, so we enter into glory through the cross.

As Christ was glorified through the cross, so we enter into glory through the cross, the glory of Christ that is far greater than any other glory we may seek.

The cross is the greatest leadership statement in history, and no leader has given more or done more for His followers than Jesus.

Often in leadership, the cross is the forgotten element because we don't connect it with leading. Discipleship, yes; leadership, no. That is where we have missed it and that is why Jesus called His followers to take up the cross. If there is no cross there is no leadership. This is Jesus' message to Peter as well as to us.

Yet Jesus issued the call of the cross to Peter, one of His most important leaders. He was preparing His men to take the message of the cross into the world; but if Peter and the disciples rejected the cross, His message had no future. Thus, Jesus demanded that they join Him in taking up the cross for their own sake and for the sake of His message.

Apart from the cross, our hands reach for a crown. Through the cross, our hands find the grace-filled power of Christ. Why would any leader settle for less?

Career and the Cross

Whether you're in business or ministry, the cross calls you to give up control of your career. Many of us give ourselves to God but hold on to our careers as the crown jewel of our lives and identity.

Think about this: The first thing Jesus did when He called Peter was to change his career, hence his identity. He does not do this with all of us. In most instances, He leaves us in the same career but changes our identity from businessperson, educator or pastor to disciple-maker and people-developer. As a result, our profession becomes the means by which He transforms others through us.

Please get this: The cross demands we release our careers to Christ. While you may operate in the world of business, you are really ambassadors for Christ bringing the power of His invisible kingdom to those who struggle in darkness.

Who's in Charge?

The cross does *not* make you a weak or passive leader. Instead it makes you stewards who follow Christ, not the champions of your careers or ministries. Your new owner is the One who makes the calls. Even when you are convinced God is a terrible businessperson directing you to do something that won't work, you do it anyway because you no longer wear the crown.

When I took up the cross for the first time, I knew nothing of being a man, a husband, a pastor, a father or a grandfather. I knew nothing of rejection and suffering; nothing of the fruit of pride or the real need for repentance.

These are the kind of things the cross reveals to us as we become Christ's leaders because without this painful process, we have nothing to offer our followers but simplistic solutions that give the pride of theology without the reality of humility. Only the cross can free us from pride.

The cross is the missing link between our inadequacy and Christ's adequacy. Make sure you grasp this point.

Leader's Disease

Jesus never stopped calling His disciples to the cross despite their resistance, but each time He brought it up, the disciples became engaged in a competition for a crown. They didn't want to hear about the cross, so they tried to drown out His words by arguing about who among them was the greatest. They were reaching for a jeweled diadem, but Jesus was giving them a handful of ugly splinters from the cross.

The disciples had Leader's Disease.

Today's leaders are just as prone to this same deadly illness. Unfortunately, it is not a condition that can be eradicated by medical research and the discovery of a vaccine.

In Scripture, we see four situations where the disciples clearly reveal its symptoms. These examples challenge us to examine our own lives to see if we, too, could have this insidious disease.

The first instance occurred in Capernaum before they began their final trip to Jerusalem (see Mark 9:33-35), the next on the road to Jerusalem (see Mark 10:32-34), then in the Upper Room at the Last

Supper (see Luke 24:14-24) and finally on the way to the Mount of Olives (see Mark 14:27-32).

A Confused Picture of Leadership

In Capernaum they were gathered together at Peter's house. Jesus asked them what they had been arguing about on the way—but they kept silent because they were ashamed of their conversation. While He was telling them that He must suffer on the cross, they were arguing over who among them was the greatest (see Mark 9:34)!

Jesus' response was surprising. He didn't rebuke them for their passion to be the greatest. He wanted them to become His great leaders and, instead, rebuked them for their confusion about true greatness. He said, "If anyone wants to be first, he shall be last of all and servant of all" (Mark 9:35). True greatness is being the last and the least, rather than being number one.

In this incident we see the first symptom of Leader's Disease:

Symptom #1: shameful competition driven by selfish ambition

These followers of Jesus, men selected by Him, showed that they were ultimately committed to themselves, not Jesus. They expected Jesus to set up His kingdom, and they wanted to rule with Him. They had not even begun to understand what lay ahead.

If you have personal competition and selfish ambition, you have Leader's Disease. I have met very few people who don't, or at least didn't start out, thinking this way.

In It for Number One

On the way to Jerusalem Jesus again brought up the cross, this time describing His crucifixion in vivid detail (Mark 10:32-34). Immediately, James and John acted to settle the issue of who the greatest was by making a shameless power play. They used their family connections against the other disciples.

> **If there are power plays in your church or business, or if you are pursuing your will in Jesus' name, you have Leader's Disease.**

Clearly, they had not grasped a word Jesus had said. They were in it for themselves. This is the second symptom of Leader's Disease:

Symptom #2: a shameless use of power to get what we want

If there are power plays in your church or business, or if you are pursuing your will in Jesus' name, you have Leader's Disease.

Insensitivity to Others

During the Passover meal in Jerusalem, Jesus and His men were gathered at the table. Jesus shared His heart with them and told them that His betrayer was one of them.

As they considered who this could be, their conversation again degenerated into a debate over who was the greatest among them (see Luke 22:14-24). No one could be more vulnerable than Jesus at this moment just before His arrest, and no one could be more insensitive than the disciples. They demonstrated the third symptom:

Symptom #3: an insensitive drivenness that blinds leaders to the vulnerability of others

To be vulnerable is to admit need, and leaders don't easily do this. If you or members of your team are afraid of vulnerability, you have Leader's Disease.

Blind to Weakness

At this point, Jesus and the Twelve took one last walk on their way to the cross as they left the Passover meal and went to Gethsemane. Jesus told them they would all fall away from Him because of His arrest.

Once again, Peter resisted Jesus, saying he would die rather than desert Him. No matter what the others did, he would never deny Him.

We can almost imagine Peter making a grand gesture, indicating all the rest would deny Jesus, but he never would. Jesus rebuked Peter, telling him that he *would* fall away that very night, no matter how strongly Peter insisted otherwise. From this we see the fourth symptom of Leader's Disease.

Symptom #4: blind self-confidence

Peter was absolutely certain he was right, yet he was totally wrong. Even worse, he was blind to how wrong he was. How many leaders have we met like this? You or your team may have this symptom, but perhaps you can't see it. After all, it is blind.

The Solitary Cure

To grow in freedom from Leader's Disease, we must do what Jesus called His followers to do when He said:

> *"…If anyone wishes to come after Me, he must deny himself, and take up his cross and follow Me."*

Through all the competition, conniving ambition, compulsive self-protection and complete self-absorption, God was working to redeem the disciples' inadequacy by His grace and make them adequate in Christ.

What He did for the disciples so long ago, He is doing for us right now. When Leader's Disease turns your life into a wreck and your leadership is in tatters, when your castles have collapsed and your hopes lie crushed beneath the rubble, when your followers reject you and your confidence flees from you, when your critics surround you and even your friends desert you, when your crown lies dented and tarnished on the ground before you, look up, look up, look up. Look up at the one thing that is still standing: the often-forgotten cross.

Rush to the cross. Grasp the cross. Take the cross on your back, and follow the Man who carried the cross on His back. To your amazement, you will find yourself seated in the heavenlies with Him.

Finally, at last, God has you where He wants you—ready for His grace to redeem your inadequacy.

Thoughts for Reflection

Think back over the recent season of your life.

- *Has the cross been firmly over your shoulder as you've leaned in to listen to His guidance on your next steps?*

- *Have you identified the symptoms of Leader's Disease you commonly suffer with?*
  1. *competition driven by selfish ambition*
  2. *the use of power to get what we want*

3. *insensitive drivenness that blinds us to the vulnerability of others*

4. *blind self-confidence*

- *Can you see that unless the cross changes leaders' hearts, the cross can never change the world?*

- *Are you willing to crucify cultural leadership in your life and live out cross-broken leadership in your work, your ministry and your home?*

- *Are you at a point where you are ready to surrender afresh to the cross?*

Make today that day. It is the only death that brings abundant life.

Take time to surrender to Jesus and the cross right now.

CHAPTER 8

YOU'VE GOT THIS

"But by the grace of God I am what I am."
(1 Corinthians 15:10)

So far, we have focused on the disciples. We've observed that although they spent considerable time with Jesus, radical dependence on Him was a challenge. Too often as leaders, we can relate.

After all, are we to truly rely on Jesus in spite of our education and constant skill development? For that answer, let's turn our attention to an apostle who had a different kind of encounter with Jesus: the apostle Paul. Whereas most of the disciples had little education, Paul was known to be one of the most brilliant men of his day. He had studied under the well-known teacher Gamaliel and was an expert in the law of God.

Despite all of this knowledge, Paul realized that he was inadequate and desperately needed the Lord in every situation. Why? Paul had a unique perspective as an outsider to the original disciples and had been broken through blindness and dreams to rely solely on the Holy Spirit. He was able to grasp his inadequacy while the disciples seemed to need frequent reminders.

As this legendary apostle demonstrates, we can never accomplish God's will without God's empowering grace. Let's see what we can learn from his example, focusing on his ministry in Corinth.

Empowered by Grace

After successfully planting churches throughout Asia Minor, Paul moved on to one of the most unlikely cities in the Roman Empire to respond to the cross. Who would have thought that God's plan was for Paul to plant a church in Corinth, a city of pagan gods, where idolatry reigned supreme, immorality permeated the very atmosphere and every evil imaginable was present?

Well, Paul knew two things about himself as he entered Corinth.

First, he did not have the resources he needed to impact the city for Christ. He says as much when he tells the Corinthians that he came to them "in weakness with fear and in much trembling" (1 Corinthians 2:3).

The man who had planted churches all over the Roman world and endured terrible persecution from Philippi to Athens knew he was weak and had much uncertainty as he entered one of the greatest—and most decadent—cities in the Empire. He knew exactly what he faced. There was no bravado, no pumping himself up, no denial that he had a task far bigger than he was.

He knew as he entered Corinth that he carried a life-death message to the Corinthians. This is why he asked himself and his readers, "Who is adequate for these things?" (1 Corinthians 2:16). He did not have the resources to penetrate Corinth with the gospel; he was simply inadequate for the task.

Have you ever been there as a leader?

Paul never tried to hide it; he never tried to talk himself into thinking he was able to change the city, nor did he ever try to make others think he was the one who was touching so many lives. To the contrary, even when he was defending his apostolic authority, as he was in 2 Corinthians, he did not assert his power. Rather, he candidly discussed his inadequacy and insisted that he did not have the resources to transform Corinth.

He never would resort to eloquence or superior wisdom (see 1 Corinthians 2:21). He knew his adequacy came from God, and that's where he gained the confidence to overcome his fear and trembling and speak out for Christ.

Getting What We Don't Deserve

The second truth Paul knew about himself was that he did not deserve to have the resources he needed to reach Corinth. He had been a persecutor, a man of violence toward Christians who incited murder against Stephen. How could he deserve to impact such a great city? He deserved judgment for his sin, not spiritual power and the recognition and influence that his ministry brought him.

Paul was aware that nothing he achieved—neither the churches he planted nor the persecution he faced—could make up for what he did to Christ as he attacked Christians. Jesus described Himself as the "Persecuted One" when he met Paul on the road to Damascus. Paul hadn't just persecuted Christians—he had persecuted *Christ*, and nothing he could do would make up for that.

Paul marveled that Jesus appeared to him and that he was appointed an apostle. He did not deserve the blessing he received to be used by Christ. Yet God was gracious, and Paul was humbled by it.

As believers, we are each tempted to take for granted what Christ did. We might have grown up in a Christian home and become familiar with the concept of God's love as we learned to "be good." Just as we have lived "good enough" lives, we tend to think we can navigate leadership by doing the right things.

He realized his complete and utter destitution outside of God's grace—and, as a result, was radically dependent on it.

This was not the case with Paul. He realized his complete and utter destitution outside of God's grace—and, as a result, was radically dependent on it.

We know this was Paul's perspective because he tells us so in two places. The first is in 1 Corinthians 15:9-10. He marvels that Jesus appeared to him and that he was appointed an apostle because he didn't deserve that privilege after persecuting the church. It was by the grace of God that he became what he was, a grace he could never deserve.

So he outworked all the other apostles—but it was not Paul who did it. The grace of God was with him; God's grace and Paul were connected at the hip, and grace aided and supported him in all he did (see 1 Corinthians 15:9-10).

Paul speaks not only of the unearned merit of saving grace, but also of the unlimited power of saving grace. Grace was his empowerment, and he didn't succeed on his own. Paul never thought of his ministry as "Paul, Inc.," as if it were his success. Instead, he saw himself as part of a company of many who were radically and desperately dependent on the resources of grace. These resources were the undeserved power of God through his weakness.

By Grace Alone

Virtually all of us who have a relationship with Jesus know we came to Him by grace, as the apostle Paul did, and that we did nothing to gain eternal life. However, many of us don't understand that we also serve Him by grace. We haven't learned that we are just as helpless to serve Christ apart from grace, as we were to receive salvation apart from grace. We think that serving Christ is up to us.

When we hit the wall of inadequacy, we often don't realize what is happening, so we dig down inside ourselves and gut it out for Jesus.

That's exactly the wrong thing to do, and we end up wearing our Christian smiles, struggling in denial, disheartened in failure, resigned to defeat.

This takes us to our next reality, one that relies on Christ's power to flow through our gifts so we can accomplish His call for us as leaders...

Principle #6: The Reality of the Redeemed Adequacy

You are made adequate by God's empowering grace.

The more I grow as a leader, the more I realize that I am not adequate to serve Christ in any way. The more strengths and skills I muster, the clearer it is that only God's grace can turn my inadequacy into His adequacy. The fact is, all ministry is of grace. It is time to give up trying to do what God's grace alone can do through us.

The Grace Channel

Grace is the means of God's power, the channel through which His power flows like a river generating hydropower for a city. Without water there is no electrical power, and without grace there is no spiritual power. Water and grace both must flow through a channel in order to generate power.

The channel that grace used to bring God's power to Paul was his weaknesses, his spiritual inadequacy and his physical limitations, even as He does today with us. And we must not forget, Paul was from an upscale neighborhood and received a coveted education. The key was that Paul saw it all as weakness. Without these limitations, God had no means of empowering Paul. Once he realized this, Paul treasured his weaknesses as the most powerful elements in his life, the one thing worth boasting about.

He chose not to assert his authority through his strengths, as others did, because his strengths did not compare with God's weakness on the cross. If this is God's weakness, think of how great God's power was that raised Christ from the dead.

A Thorn in the Flesh

In Corinth, Paul's apostolic authority was under attack because his preaching centered on Christ's cross and not on man's wisdom. To the Corinthians, he was an unimpressive communicator, and they rejected his leadership.

Paul wrote his second letter to the Corinthians to defend his authority, but how does he defend it? Through his weakness. Who else would defend his authority by asserting his weakness?

He tells us why he did this in 2 Corinthians 12:7. The passage states that God gave him a thorn in the flesh to keep him from becoming proud, apparently a difficult physical illness that he prayed three times for God to remove.

Finally, he received an answer: God's grace was sufficient to accomplish His purposes through Paul's weakness (see verses 8-9).

Without thorns and our weaknesses, God can never accomplish His aims in our lives, and when we work to cover up our weaknesses and establish our authority through our strength, we build blocks that dam up the flow of grace in our hearts and cut off God's power through us. When Paul wrote to assert his authority, he knew he had a choice: He could either rely on Corinthian strength or Christ's weakness.

He chose Christ's weakness because he, of all people, knew it was far more powerful than Corinthian strength.

Like Paul, do you see that you neither have the resources you need to serve Christ nor that you deserve them? Do you understand that without your weaknesses and inadequacies, you have no channel for grace to bring you God's power? It is time to be grateful for your weaknesses. They are the channel for God's all-sufficient grace.

Burned Out and Broken

As leaders, we often spend our lives desperately seeking significance, not knowing how adequate we are, striving and driven to get what we already have: Christ's adequacy.

I know what I'm talking about because I've been there. Early in my ministry I was invited by a man I greatly admired to be part of a team of six men to go to the Philippines to "teach a nation." We would blanket the country teaching the principles of Ephesians 4:7-16.

Little did I know that this invitation would end in burnout and my first taste of brokenness, nor that it would take years for me to understand what God was teaching me through this experience: that I did not understand His grace.

I was much too young for such a great task, much too in need of success and recognition, much too unaware that God loved me and that I did not have to do anything to earn His love. So instead of going to serve others, I went to serve myself by showing everyone how significant I was. While on the trip and after I got home, I felt I failed and I'm sure I did, although God's word did not fail.

Because I felt so strongly that I had failed, I also felt God would fire me, that He was finished with me, that anyone who failed the way I did should be fired. Certainly that's what I would do with a failure: fire him, finish him off, pack him up and send him on his way. I did not realize that I needed God's grace to find my way out of my confusion, and I did not know God was finally getting me in the place where He could use me. Much to my amazement, God didn't fire me. Instead, He opened up doors for me I never could imagine.

When I was in this season of struggle, I read C. S. Lewis' work, *Mere Christianity*, and realized for the first time that the need to be superior by comparison and competition has its root in pride. When we try to prove to ourselves and others that we are adequate and then become disheartened because we're not, we're proud.

I am totally accepted by God. He is never finished with me, and He will never fire me.

The one thing that pride did for me was bring me to God's grace through brokenness. You see, God didn't fire me or treat me the way I would have treated others. Instead, He led me to repent and rebuild what I had torn down, showing me that He turns my inadequacy into His adequacy through His grace. Yes, amazing grace—not only for salvation, but also for service and for freedom from the bondage of self.

Living Beyond the Fear Factor

Because God loves me, I don't have to be afraid of Him. I certainly fear Him as I come to Him in worship; but I have confidence and security in His love and I am able to draw near, knowing that I am totally accepted by God. He is never finished with me, and He will never fire me. When we sin, we must not be afraid to come to Him, owning and confessing our sin.

Like Paul, I have known much fear and trembling. I am learning that I am not adequate to serve Christ in any way. Only God's grace can turn our inadequacy into His adequacy. God will do it if we will repent of the futility of our efforts to make ourselves somebody and allow His grace to freely flow through us to work His power in us. We must stop trying to do what God's grace alone can do through us.

God Loves Leaders

It's a simple but important truth: God loves leaders with an unfailing love—even when we fail—and we do not have to prove anything to anyone. If God is for us, who can be against us? If only we could—or would—act out of that truth, our leadership would take on a whole new life, the life of Christ Himself.

How *can* God love us? We can't deserve it; we can't earn it so we don't believe it—no matter what our theology tells us. Our psychology won't allow us to trust God enough to let Him love us because we feel we must figure out a way to be worthy of His love. We do not understand God's grace.

When we see the ways of God in leader formation, we discover that it's the intangibles of His love and grace that make leadership effective, and the lifetime pilgrimage leaders pursue to grow in these realities is what makes their leadership increasingly complete. God's love and grace enable altared-heart leaders to exercise exceptional leadership.

The Holy Spirit constantly and insistently speaks truth into our lives with the deepest insight possible. Yet the Holy Spirit is also our comforter, the one sent to take Christ's personal place in our lives. We see this especially as leaders when we fail and experience His encouraging presence within us.

Why do we often struggle and become depressed when we feel like we fail—or actually *do* fail? Why do we measure ourselves by the success of others or by a self-imposed standard we pursue because it makes us feel like we are the best? Do you realize that competition is pride and that our pride is a dam—an obstacle for God's grace?

He simply loves us. Even when we fail Him, even when we expect things of ourselves that He never expected of us, He still loves us. No one deserves it, yet everyone has it—even those who reject it.

"If God is for us, who is against us?" (Romans 8:31). If only we could—or would—act out of this truth, our leadership would take on a whole new life: the life of Christ Himself.

Wholeness in Him

As we go through brokenness, God brings wholeness into our lives by pouring His healing and enabling grace into the places where we are broken. Our eyes are opened, our ears are unstopped, our minds are transformed and our hands are released.

> **Once you've experienced His empowering grace, you will never want to settle for less.**

Now we lead the way Jesus led because He leads through us. Now others follow us as never before, with commitment and conviction because they see Christ in us. We are no longer broken leaders because we are made whole through grace.

The empowering grace of the cross delivers us from futile self-dependence to the enablement of Christ-dependence. Once you've experienced His empowering grace, you will never want to settle for less.

Thoughts for Reflection

Paul sees his weakness as channels of God's power by His grace.

- *What weaknesses do you have that could be channels of God's powerful grace through you?*

- *Have you seen your weaknesses in this way, or are you still praying for God to take them away as Paul once did?*

- *What if He doesn't? How can you glory in those weaknesses so His grace can flow through you into the lives of others? Be specific in giving your answer.*

- *What would you say is your "thorn in the flesh"?*

- *What failures do you need to reassess in the light of His grace?*

Take some time and thank God for his love and grace that you could never earn, but that He freely lavishes on you. Ask Him to forgive you for trying to carry your leadership burden on your own. Lay it at His feet. Accept His grace as your sole source of power for living and leading for Him.

CHAPTER 9

IT'S NOT ABOUT YOU

"Let this mind be in you which was also in Christ Jesus."
(Philippians 2:5 - NKJV)

As the time draws near for Jesus' crucifixion, He heads to Gethsemane with three of His beloved disciples to pray. Even though Jesus has the cross on His mind, the leadership lessons are in full session. The disciples, of course, are oblivious to what's at hand and cannot stay awake after the Passover feast—¬even in spite of Jesus' words beforehand, "My soul is exceedingly sorrowful, even to death" (Matthew 27:38). Their lack of empathy does not deter Jesus, however. He knows the critical nature of time spent with His Father.

The fact that Jesus' prayers are recorded in Scripture should cause us to take note. What can we learn from them? And how can Gethsemane change us as modern-day leaders?

"If it is Possible, Let This Cup Pass from Me"

There are no words to describe what Jesus must have felt as He shared a Passover meal with His disciples. After breaking bread with them—and predicting Peter's denial—Jesus went with Peter, James and John to Gethsemane, a garden located at the foot of the Mount of Olives.

The Gospel of Matthew indicates that Jesus was "sorrowful" and "deeply distressed" (26:37).

Here in Gethsemane, Jesus spent time praying to the Father, knowing that He would soon be crucified. Three times, He asked God, if possible, to "let this cup pass from Me" (verses 39-42). This was not any ordinary prayer time. Throughout history, numerous artists have illustrated this scene, referring to it as "Agony in the Garden."

As Jesus prayed, his distress was beyond Him. He needed the support of those He counted on the most while He sought out the One who had been His support through His earthly pilgrimage.

It was His Father who called Jesus to do what He was doing, who would sustain Him in this moment. Yet, with all the encouragement His Father could give Him, Jesus still wanted the support of His three friends, Peter, James and John. This is not a charade, not play-acting for our benefit, not the strong one pretending He is weak to make the children feel good. This is real, as real as our Gethsemanes are when we call on others to help us when we feel as if we are going to die. Nothing shows His humanity more clearly than His time in Gethsemane.

Embracing the Bigger Prize

From Gethsemane, Jesus went to Golgotha—from the struggle of "yes" to the reality of the cross. He endured suffering that is beyond our imagination: physically, spiritually and emotionally.

You see, it wasn't only the physical pain; it was the spiritual reality of all the sin of humanity for all of history being put on Him. It was the isolation of facing this totally alone without His Father to support Him because neither the Spirit nor the Father could stand with Him in the weight of that sin.

The essence of judgment is separation from God—that is what death means for all who do not respond to God's grace, and that is what the cross meant for Jesus when He became sin for us (2 Corinthians 5:21).

His unbroken fellowship with the Father broken on the cross was what made Him cry out, "My God, My God, why have You forsaken Me?" (Matthew 27:46). He knew why God turned away, but the pain of His isolation forced that cry from His lips.

In our most difficult moments of facing self, we can never know anything as shameful as the cross. Yet He looked down on that shame seeing it as nothing compared to the thought of having us with Him. What stunning love made Jesus drink the cup He wanted to escape? Instead, He willingly accepted it for our sake! What glory was there in that cup of death? Every kind of unimaginable glory in heaven and on earth!

It was on that cross that God began to answer His Son's prayer for His restored glory (see John 17:1-5). As life ebbed out of Him, His restored glory flowed into Him. In that moment of death when

Nicodemus and Joseph of Arimathia took Him down from the cross, they were carrying the glory of God.

Out of the darkness of our desperation comes a glory we never imagined: resurrection glory.

As they carried Jesus' body to the brand-new tomb, wrapped it in linen and spices, and laid it on the death shelf, they thought they were burying the dead remains of Jesus. Little did they know that they had just handled the glory of God, that in three days time that body would come back to life as the glorified body of the Savior. Little did they grasp that they had just carried the all-powerful Grace of God with full resurrection resources for all who trust in Him.

And little do we know that when we take up our cross and face our fading glory, we are entering into the greatest glory possible. Out of the darkness of our desperation comes a glory we never imagined: resurrection glory. It rarely comes in three days or three weeks or even three years, but it will come; and when it comes, it's far greater than we could ever imagine.

Could we have greater hope? The way to this hope always goes through Gethsemane and the cross. When we fear the shame of sin and the cross in our lives, we are fearing the greatest hope we have—

forgiveness and restoration that comes when we empty ourselves, humble ourselves and sacrifice ourselves in Christ's will.

And this leads to the last principle of an altared leader...

Principle #7:
The Reality of Radical Sacrifice

You must do what Jesus did: empty yourself,
humble yourself, and sacrifice yourself..

The Mind of Christ

When Jesus commanded His leaders and followers to take up the cross and follow Him, this is what He was talking about. He knew He was asking them to give up everything. He did not make it optional; rather, He made it central to leadership. It was central not only to the formation of the early disciples that would lead the greatest movement in history, but also to His Church throughout the ages. He directed us to live as He lived and to take up our cross the way He took up His cross.

How did He do this, and how can we learn to take up our cross from Him? Philippians 2:5-8 answers these questions. To live His way, we must have His mind and make three decisions Jesus made in taking up the cross.

First, He **emptied Himself**—not of His deity, but of the visible expression of His glory and the freedom to pursue His own will. Instead, he submitted Himself to His Father and gave up all of His rights as God. He determined to have no will of His own, only His Father's will for Him, which was to take up the cross.

Second, **He humbled Himself** *by becoming obedient unto death*. Jesus, who had known only co-equal sovereignty with the Father and the Spirit, became subordinate to both. He did nothing except what the Father wanted and the Spirit directed Him to do (see John 6:38).

Third, He **sacrificed Himself**—*"even death on a cross"* (Philippians 2:8). In these words, Paul expressed his amazement that Jesus, God's equal, would die in such a demeaning and shameful way; but He did it willingly because it was the Father's will and His own heart for us.

So to follow Jesus means we do as He did through Him: We empty ourselves, humble ourselves and sacrifice ourselves. This is the mind of Christ.

How do we have the mind of Christ? The Jesus way. Plain and simple, there are no shortcuts.

- *First, we **empty ourselves** of all our rights*, especially our self-centered rights that give root to our drivenness: our right to success, to recognition, to dignity, to value. We let go of any right that, when infringed upon, makes us resentful or angry.

> **...to follow Jesus means we do as He did through Him: We empty ourselves, humble ourselves and sacrifice ourselves.**

As leaders we must willfully empty ourselves of self-interest in an act of trust in Jesus. We release ourselves to Him, even as He did to the Spirit and the Father. We empty ourselves of all drives for glory, all striving for self-protection, all schemes for personal advancement and every dimension of self we can discern.

In doing this we will discover that self reaches much deeper in us than we realized, that it is subtle in deceptive ways we never imagined and that each new turn in life reveals a new dimension of self we were utterly unaware of.

We need to recognize we often are driven by desires for personal success in the name of Jesus and have been blinded by our drive for power and missed seeing it entirely. We discover we have been threatened by other leaders and undermined them in the name of

Jesus, sometimes without knowing it and sometimes knowing it full well.

The mind of Christ calls for us to empty ourselves as He did and be the kind of follower He became so we can become the kind of Leader He is. This is why we need to understand that taking up the cross is a process of repeatedly placing our hearts on God's altar.

- *Next, we must **humble ourselves** by becoming obedient.* How does a proud man humble himself? By becoming obedient to God against his will.

While Jesus was Lord of all, He voluntarily became the most humiliated of all. As leaders, the last thing many of us want is to be held accountable; however, obedience to God virtually always includes human accountability. Part of taking up the cross demands submission to the authority God places over us, which, in our minds, may be improper and unqualified—yet God uses the blunt and painful tools of accountability to form us into cross-bearers.

- *Finally, we **sacrifice ourselves** through death, even death on the cross.* For Jesus this was an act of love toward us; for us this is a painful struggle. It means we give up everything that matters to us, everything that we draw on for identity: our vision, hopes, plans, gifts, treasures, time—everything. A day has to come when we put all on the cross and release it to the grave and let the Father raise what He will.

Unless we take up our cross and die, we will always be dead in the power of sin and self. Sacrificing ourselves means we die to our expectations and false identities, the masks we wear to hide ourselves from others and keep others from us.

Through this sacrifice, we understand our identification with Christ and realize that as He hung on the cross, we were there with Him. We discover that through taking up the cross, we enter into the freedom to lead that we so desperately seek.

When we take up the cross, we experience death and find the birth of life in our leadership. We discover the life of radical sacrifice and realize we have been trading it for a life of death and self.

As leaders, the cross redeems our inadequacy and transforms our insufficiency into Christ's sufficiency. When we make the radical sacrifice of thinking His way, we make the only decision that ultimately brings sense to life because it is the only decision that delivers us from true leadership death to leadership life.

Living Selfless

The decision to empty ourselves, humble ourselves and sacrifice ourselves is not a one-time decision, but one that we make many times.

We find ourselves in Gethsemane with Christ repeatedly because it is through the garden of struggle that we move to our personal

Golgotha. Gethsemane will not be a constant experience for us, but there will be Gethsemane seasons throughout our lives when we face overwhelming cups we don't want to drink. The cross moves deeper and deeper into our hearts, freeing us from the hidden folds of self.

When we come to Gethsemane with our Lord, we see Him as He enters new depths of emptying Himself. He was uncommonly vulnerable on this night as He spoke to His disciples. Now He pours out His very soul to them and asks them to stand guard with Him and pray with Him.

How much more can He empty Himself than to turn for support to those who would desert Him that very night? Selah.

Our Gethsemane

There will be times when this is what Gethsemane means for us: struggle, confusion, injustice, pain, anguish, isolation. This is where we must go to empty ourselves and take up the cross in deeper and deeper ways. This is when we must say yes when we want to say no.

Hebrews 5:7 tells us it was because of reverent submission that God heard His prayer. Somehow, answered prayer for Jesus depended on His "reverent submission" to the Father. If that is what it took for Jesus to get prayer answered, what does it take for us?

We can only enter into His spirit of submission and obedience through Him, and only He can enable us to pray and humble ourselves in such a way that our prayer is answered.

Only leaders who say "yes" when they want to say "no" enter into Christ's kind of leadership; the rest do leadership things while satisfying their fleshly desires for power, success and control and bearing the fruit this brings. It's no wonder that the Spirit ultimately unmasks them for the failures and phonies they truly are.

There remains one last aspect to the radical decision we must make through the mind of Christ.

Laying It Down

> **Our salvation meant His life for our lives; true leadership means our lives for His life.**

Jesus humbled Himself by becoming obedient to death—even death on a cross. He sacrificed Himself for us. Saying "yes" when He wanted to say "no" cost Jesus His life; He made the ultimate sacrifice for our sake.

Now He calls us to make the ultimate sacrifice for His sake. Our salvation meant His life for our lives; true leadership means our lives for His life.

To lead His way, we must give up our lives—our wills, our plans, our expectations and our self for His will, His plan, His expectations and the self He has for us. We enter into His kind of leadership when we choose to make His kind of decision to do His will no matter what it costs.

Most of us have made this decision already—thus, we know how subtle self can be, how deceptive our hearts are, how easily we find ourselves doing what we don't want to do. We are taken captive as prisoners of war in the battle with sin. We realize that when we think we have made that sacrifice—and we may have—our flesh sneaks up on us and trips us up once again.

Proud thoughts flood our minds as we prepare to communicate for Christ; drivenness propels us into anger when our way is blocked; unjust criticism disheartens us and makes us want to quit.

Gethsemane beckons and calls us to the cup once again. It's time to take up the cross in ways we thought we already had. There's yet another dimension of self to deny, another time we need to say "yes" to the Father when we want to say "no."

Will this never end? No!

Our Gethsemanes will only end when we face the final "yes" of death and enter into the eternal glory of Christ. The cup is not constant, but we will never stop entering the garden as long as we live. Old dimensions of death never end, even as new dimensions of life are ever beginning. This is the leader's life, the pathway to leadership in Christ, the pathway to ultimate joy in Him.

When It Happens

The seasons we find ourselves in Gethsemane are never convenient. This was the case for a dear friend whose life—and business—took on a whole new dimension when he laid down his plans for God's perfect plan.

After working for decades to create the business and lifestyle he envisioned, this businessman gradually lost 90% of his business. A team of over 300 employees quickly shrank to 30, while his tremendous overhead costs stayed constant.

He sought the Lord and discovered he needed to deal with three issues: deep, unacknowledged sin he had to be delivered from; fears the Lord wanted him to face; and the decision to run his business God's way rather than his way.

He faced the sin, struggling and wrestling, and gradually gained such freedom that he since became a model for other men who now seek him out for discipleship. He then focused on his fears and found release from them. After dealing with these issues, his business started to grow again.

About eighteen months later, however, he came to me again and said he had lost 60% of his business. So he went back to the Lord and made a challenging discovery: He realized that he had not fully submitted His business to the Lord. Wholeheartedly, he asked God to take his identity, his control, his success and everything that mattered to him.

He emptied himself, humbled himself and sacrificed himself on the altar of the cross. In fact, he put everything in the grave and told God to raise what He wanted. What was the result of this decision? Resurrection! And when God resurrects something in our lives, He brings it back glorified.

Today, his business thrives. He has built a strong support team for his organization, which gives him freedom to rest and serve in ministry more than ever. He is one of the finest disciplers that I have ever seen. He is a mentor of many and sought-out by other leaders who want to learn from him. His transformation even translated into tremendous spiritual growth in his family.

Who could possibly not want this kind of fruit in life? Yet, it was this leader's personal death that truly led to Christ's life through him. What a paradox!

Of course, it is frightening to entrust everything to God, but will the One who sent His Son to die for us not "graciously give us all things"? (Romans 8:32).

Christ's Kind of Leader

It is time for leaders to do what Jesus called us to do: deny ourselves, take up our cross and follow Him through Gethsemane to the cross.

To follow Him, we must have His mind so we can make His choices and say "yes" when we want to say "no." The more we rely on the sufficiency of sacrifices we made long ago, the more self-deceived we are. The more aware we are of the need to return to Gethsemane, the more likely we are to become Christ's kind of leader.

In a day and age when much of the appeal to Christian leaders is an appeal to lead as the world leads, we must decide to do what Jesus did: empty ourselves, humble ourselves and sacrifice ourselves in Christ's power. This is the radical decision we have to make, and the time to make it is now.

> *Now unto Him who is able to do exceedingly abundantly beyond all we can ask or think according to the power the mightily works within us...*
>
> *— the Apostle Paul, Ephesians 3:20*

Thoughts for Reflection

The same Jesus who told us to give up our lives and carry our cross told us He came to give us abundant life.

- *Are you willing to trust Him that He has your best interests in mind?*

- *Are you willing to put on the mind of Christ?*

- *Are you willing to empty yourself? What must you let go of?*

- *Are you willing to humble yourself? What act of obedience is God asking of you?*

- *Are you willing to sacrifice yourself as you follow Him? What will that entail?*

- *Are you willing to put everything in the grave and see what God will raise?*

Taking up the cross, as Jesus commanded, is not the mere burden of calling ourselves believers—it is the radial sacrifice of our lives and our will for His. Are you willing to take up the cross? When we sacrifice our desires for His sake, their death produces immeasurable glory.

Now is the time. Trust God to show you that trusting Him in such a radical way bears the most positive fruit possible. If you are struggling with this decision, cry out to God right now to enable you to do what He wants you to do. If you can, include others (perhaps those you lead) in your Gethsemane moment. Over time, it will produce glorified fruit in you and in the lives of those around you.

CHAPTER 10

WHAT IS GOD FORMING IN YOU?

"…He will teach you all things, and bring to your remembrance all that I said to you." (John 14:26)

What would it look like if we let Christ form us the way he formed the disciples? What if we walked in the mind of Christ? What if we truly emptied ourselves, humbled ourselves and sacrificed ourselves?

That is what Jesus called His leaders to do. When they did, they impacted nations and set the world ablaze with the gospel.

This was no small feat. Jesus shaped twelve men in three years to change the world. And when He left this earth, He left them and us with the Holy Spirit. As the promise of the Holy Spirit was given believers, we are reminded that the Holy Spirit would give power for us to live like Christ—He would bring to our remembrance the things that Jesus taught.

What Jesus taught was more than just the beatitudes and his public teachings, it was also the real life lessons and transformative challenges He gave His disciples. He taught the disciples, and ultimately us, the seven realities of leader formation…

Principle #1:
The Reality of Leader Inadequacy

You must do what you cannot do with what you do not have for the rest of your life.

Principle #2:
The Reality of Christ's Adequacy

Jesus can do what you cannot do for the rest of your life.

Principle #3:
The Reality of the Hardened Heart

Your heart is the heart of the matter.

Principle #4:
The Reality of the Misfocused Mind

Left to yourself, you will pursue your will in Jesus' name.

Principle #5:
The Reality of the Forgotten Cross

Your death means life for your leadership.

Principle #6:
The Reality of Redeemed Adequacy

You are made adequate by God's empowering grace.

Principle #7:
The Reality of the Radical Sacrifice

You must do what Jesus did: empty yourself, humble yourself and sacrifice yourself.

The realities that Christ conveyed to His disciples are now passed to you and me as leaders in this age. Will we die for Him as He died for us? Will we trust Him in death as He trusted His Father in death?

Will we take all our expectations that bring us identity and all our achievements that bring us our security apart from Him, and release them to Him? Will we recognize that apart from His power is self, and that self must be denied if we are to find our true identity and security? Will we actually follow Him as leaders?

> **...you must take your expectations and consciously yield them to Him by taking up your cross and following Him.**

What future do you want? The one you are slaving and struggling to carve out for yourself to show everyone that you deserve a crown, or the one that the cross will bring you—the one that Jesus offers you through your death into His life?

If you want His kind of future—a future of moving from glory to glory, a future of exalting Him and transforming others—then you must take your expectations and consciously yield them to Him by taking up your cross and following Him.

Take every expectation, every thought, whether purposeful or idle, and release it to Him. Place all of the dreams, visions, drives and desires that make you who you are and keep you going, that give you hope for the future, and release them to Him.

Make Disciples of <u>All</u> the Nations

This radical sacrifice is as much a part of the Great Commission as going and telling. Making disciples means that we lead others to give up all for the sake of Christ. We often fail to accomplish the Great Commission by denying the totality of its demand. The Great Commission costs more than we're willing to pay. We often struggle to see that Jesus gave us the utterly unspectacular and painful way of the cross as the *only* way we can penetrate our world. It's as slow as lava and just as unstoppable.

This is where we meet the wall of inadequacy because, even though we can't form such leaders, this is what Jesus commanded us to do. To fail in this is to disobey Him. It is true that we can't—but *He* can as He works through us when we trust Him, and He left us a process we can implement as we abide in Him.

Take note that Jesus did not change His men. He created an environment in which change could occur, but His men chose to change—and not all of them did. We too can build an environment through Him in which the heart can be altared and lives transformed.

Below I present ten change actions that will help you create an environment for leader formation in those you lead.

1. Commit to obey Christ and form leaders in the hand of Christ.

This may be the most frightening decision you ever make. You might be a leader who fears being known so you keep people at a distance, but you cannot phone in the leader formation process. Jesus calls for you to obey Him, and you cannot allow fear of your followers to stop you from obeying your Lord.

On the other hand, you might be a businessperson who never thought you could form a leader. You must understand that the ultimate measurement of your life lies in the leaders you form, not in the money you give. Take the resurrection risk of trusting Jesus to do what He can do through you.

2. Emphasize God, not you.

We are never the issue when it comes to forming leaders. Jesus knew that and said as much when He declared He had accomplished God's will by making Him known to the disciples (see John 17:1-10). Our task is to turn all our followers' attention to God: His promises, His presence, His purpose and His power. Don't worry about you: what you can or can't do, what you're afraid of or feel confident in doing. We truly don't matter in this process. Seek God and you will find Him.

Then share what you are learning through the leader formation process with those you are serving, and you will see Him begin

> **Don't worry about you: what you can or can't do, what you're afraid of or feel confident in doing. We truly don't matter in this process.**

to form them into leaders right in front of you. What could be greater? And remember when you focus on God, focus on His grace. Make sure they know the God of grace who makes His resources available to all and will lead His way.

3. Focus on God's Word.

Everything Jesus did was based on God's Word—from His self-awareness that He had to fulfill all righteousness to be the Messiah, to His response when tempted, to His answers about His death and, later, His resurrection. Jesus created an environment in which His disciples lived and breathed God's Word. This is one of the things that attracted them to Him, as they were well aware of God's truth and wanted to know it better.

4. Immerse yourself and your emerging leaders in prayer.

No one in Scripture prayed as much as Jesus, and although we don't have a complete record of His prayers, we do know from John 17 that He prayed for two things: Himself and His disciples.

Theologian Haddon Robinson has said, "Prayer is the battle, and ministry is the taking of the spoils." In Christ's leadership, nothing happened apart from prayer. Can it be any different in ours? I am convinced that prayer was the greatest transformation instrument in Christ's leader formation, the one element that contributed most to His altared heart environment.

5. Build on the foundation of emerging relationships.

Jesus had only three years to accomplish His God-assigned task, yet He took one year to sort out the men He met before making His final choice. He had to choose a few from the many, and He weighed His decision most carefully. So must we.

When it comes time to invite others to join in your pilgrimage with you, think carefully, pray faithfully and select wisely. You may not like some of the followers you feel compelled to select, but that's not important. Draw your potential leaders from your responsive relationships as Jesus did.

6. Provide growth opportunities.

Jesus took His men everywhere He could with Him—into teaching situations, controversy, response and rejection, stress, tension, reaction—and showed them how to lead in every circumstance they would ever face. There's no record that He lectured them very much about leadership, mostly that He modeled how to respond to both opportunity and opposition. We can teach truth and train skills, but the only way followers become leaders is if they see a leader in action. Knowing theory helps, but only in a limited way. Leaders who only know theory become theoretical leaders, and theoretical leaders cannot meet the demands of reality. Take the risk of forming real leaders.

7. Be vulnerable.

Vulnerability is the most demanding requirement for leader-formers, and it cannot be avoided. It transports leadership from theory into reality and makes the leader real to the followers.

> **Vulnerability is the most demanding requirement for leader-formers, and it cannot be avoided.**

No one in Scripture was more vulnerable than Jesus on the night of His arrest in the Upper Room or Gethsemane or on the cross. Few studies are more enlightening than the study of Paul's autobiographical statements, which show him to be a humble, dependent man in need of support, as well as a man who struggled with sin in his life in deep ways. He never quite recovered from his persecution of the church; he never got past the wonder that Jesus saved him and made him an apostle. Undoubtedly, his vulnerability is what made him so attractive to his followers and enabled him to build vital teams and attract such strong leaders.

If you want to attract committed followers to join with you in serving Christ, you must follow the lead of our Lord and His chief apostle.

8. Model the cross.

The essence of this book is about overcoming the wall of inadequacy by taking up the cross and discovering wholeness through brokenness. Everyone who does this will become an influencer of others, a leader because leadership is the fruit of vulnerability.

Show your disciples what it looks like to say "no" to a crown and "yes" to the cross, and you will show them how to lead. If they have leadership gifts, they will find them and use them even as Peter and James and John did, each in his own way.

Sure, you can show them how to use their skills or send them to someone who is a better skill mentor for them than you are, but you are their model for brokenness and the cross—the most important leadership requirement of all.

9. Guide through death into life.

Taking up the cross is death for the self. The ego wants to assert itself, not die; the self wants to express itself, not deny itself. Death in any form is painful and dark, and we desperately need help when we pass through it.

People in pain often bring pain to others, and you must help them understand why they are suffering, why it is normal to hurt and grieve, how they can let go of the death they have been carrying for so long, what their new glory looks like, how it will last for eternity and what a great future lies before them as they give up the old and receive the new by grace. But you can only do this if you have passed from death to life yourself—and know you must do it many times in life. If you are not vulnerable and willing to take them on your journey with you, they will never invite you to go on theirs with them.

10. Be patient—even when your followers are frustrating.

Jesus found His followers to be frustrating at times, debating who was the greatest among themselves or degenerating into an argument with the Pharisees about casting out demons.

"How long must I be with you?" He asked them one day. Yet He stayed with them, even with Judas up until the last minute, doing everything He could to transform the traitor before He released him to do his evil deed.

Forming leaders is a long, slow process. Just when you feel you've done it, your best candidate fails. You quit in discouragement, only to see him blossom into more than you thought he could ever become years later. Or your least likely candidate becomes an amazing leader when you're not looking.

Never give up on a leader until, like Judas, he gives you no other choice.

Thoughts for Reflection

The heart of the leader is the heart of leadership. Only a heart that allows God to actively form it can overcome the wall of inadequacy, put down the crown and take up the cross and discover God's unexpected, redeeming grace.

This is altared heart leadership, the only kind of leadership that delivers us from the dead and brings us into resurrection power.

This is the kind of leader Jesus wants to form through you even as He forms you into that kind of leader.

> *"If anyone wishes to come after Me, he must deny himself, and take up his cross and follow Me" (Matthew 16:24).*

Now it's our turn. It's our turn to face our leadership afresh with new eyes and a new heart. It's our turn to take up the cross.

- *What will life as an altared leader produce in you? In the lives of those you lead?*

- *What will it mean in your life to trust God, not only in physical death, but also with the loss of control?*

- *What if God has a different future for you than the one you've built your ultimate identity on? Do you fear the potential loss of identity or significance?*

- *What does God want you to put in the grave and trust Him to raise in His will and time? How does it make you feel to release your success so totally to Him?*

- *What will it mean for you to give up your expectation and accept His? Remember this: Whatever God wants in our lives is for His glory and our good, so having the mind of Christ at work in us is the greatest thing that could ever happen to us.*

- *If you are an older leader and know you are holding on to power for your own sense of identity in the name of Jesus, when will you put that drive in the grave? Or will you take it to the grave with you?*

- *How will you build into the lives of others? How can you share your journey of leader formation with them? Who are you supposed to mentor through this process?*

Plan and take specific steps to release your leadership to others and mentor them to become greater leaders than you could ever be.

Thank you for answering the call to be a leader for Christ and for opening your heart to begin this journey.

My prayer is that you will fully step into the spiritual formation process, recognizing that what Christ desires to form in you is always the paramount issue. May you find your strength in the weakness of God and the humility of Christ through the Spirit's power—for the sake of those you lead, to multiple generations.